NEW AGE
versus
THE GOSPEL

Christianity's
Greatest Challenge

DAVID MARSHALL

Introduction
JOHN STOTT

AUTUMN
HOUSE

DAVID MARSHALL

David Marshall took Honours in Modern History and
Politics at Hull University. Thereafter he undertook
post-graduate research under Professor J. P. Kenyon at
Hull, Cambridge and London culminating
in a PhD in History.

The Devil Hides Out, Dr. Marshall's first book on the
occult, became a best seller on both sides of the
Atlantic. *Where Jesus Walked* and *Battle for the Book*
have become classics.

An internationally published Christian journalist,
Dr. Marshall is widely known in evangelical circles. He
is also an editor, teacher and well-known public
speaker. He lives in Lincolnshire with his wife,
and is part of a large, three-tier family.

Cover photograph
ACE/Chris Yates

Copyright © Autumn House
First published 1993

ISBN 1 873796 22 6

Published by Autumn House
Alma Park, Grantham, Lincs., NG31 9SL, England

Introduction by
JOHN STOTT
Rector Emeritus, All Souls, Langham Place, London.

Conflicting gospels

The New Age movement is misnamed because it is neither an organized movement, nor the harbinger of a new age, in spite of its claim.

It is, however, an uneasy blend of Eastern mysticism and Western materialism, of science and superstition, of physics and metaphysics, of ancient wisdom and new consciousness, and its ideas are seeping into our culture through the media, through science fiction, through schools, colleges and business courses.

At the risk of over-simplification I can find three basic concepts that give unity to that cluster of ideas.

First, **All is one.** This is a fundamental tenet of Hinduism, that the individual self or soul is the universal self or soul. The New Age movement has borrowed it. In other words, in spite of appearances to the contrary, there are no real distinctions between God and human beings, us and others, persons and things, you and me, and even good and evil. Instead, all these are manifestations of the same single reality.

Secondly, **All is God.** Shirley MacLaine, whom one might describe as the high priestess of the New Age movement, writes that there is 'one basic spiritual law' which would make the world 'a happier, healthier place', and that is that 'everyone is god — everyone'.

So the good news of the New Age movement is 'You are god and I am god and all human beings are god.' In her book *Dancing in the Light* Ms MacLaine says: 'I know that I exist, therefore I am. I know that the godsource exists, therefore it is. Since I am part of that force, I am that I am.' She thus takes upon herself the Divine title.

In the view of the New Age movement the basic human predicament is not moral (sin and guilt) but metaphysical (ignorance of our true identity). The alienation which human beings experience is not alienation from God but from our true selves. What we need, therefore, is not forgiveness but enlightenment. Salvation (although they do not use the word) comes not from without — somebody coming to our rescue — but from within. In other words, salvation is finding myself.

Thirdly, the New Age movement believes that **All is well**. Its followers are convinced that the New Age will bring an era of peace, harmony and happiness. They see themselves as standing on the very threshold of the millennium. Because human beings are gods, we have an unlimited potential for personal transformation.

It would be easy for Christians to dismiss New Age thinking as a naïve and harmless aberration. But it has to be taken seriously.

From beginning to end the New Age movement expresses a preoccupation, even an infatuation with self. It puts self in the place of God and even declares that we *are* God.

New Agers have surrendered to the primeval temptation to become like God. God is effectively dethroned. The New Age movement dispenses with the Trinity.

First, it dispenses with God the Father, the transcendental creator, by identifying Him with the universe.

But it is essential for us to distinguish the creation from its creator and to affirm our creaturely dependence on Him.

Secondly, the New Age movement dispenses with God the Son, our unique Redeemer. Our human predicament is not ignorance, but sin. The solution to it lies not inside ourselves but outside.

The true good news is not that I can awaken to my true self as being divine, but that Christ Jesus came into the world to save sinners.

Thirdly, the New Age movement dispenses with God the Holy Spirit, our indwelling sanctifier.

To New Agers 'transformation' has nothing to do with people's morality or behaviour. It refers rather to the transformation of their consciousness, the discovery and development of their own potential.

So we have to choose between two incompatible gospels. On the one hand there is the false gospel of the New Age movement which centres on 'me', on my identity and my potentiality. On the other hand there is the true Gospel which centres on God — on the Father who loves us, the Son who died for us, and the Spirit who indwells and transforms us.

There is no possibility of compromise between these two Gospels. The true new age was inaugurated by Jesus Christ at His first coming. The so-called 'New Age' movement is both a counterfeit and a fraud.

JOHN R. W. STOTT

'Conflicting Gospels' by John Stott was first given as a talk at All Souls and is available on audio cassette from All Souls Tape Library, 2 All Souls Place, London, W1N 3DB.

Contents

Upfront

Gurus fly West on one-way tickets. Youth from the West fly East in search of gurus. India, rich in resources and manpower, yet where millions are malnourished and live in poverty, has become both the source and centre of a new movement that aspires to become a new world religion.

An Indian journalist working in London describes his country as 'a wounded civilization, paralysed by its religious beliefs'. Nevertheless, for a quarter of a century now, those beliefs and the Hindu guru godmen who expound them, and all the yoga-meditation paraphernalia that goes with them, has proved irresistible to a Western world in the grip of radical materialism.

Rabindrinaf Maharaj, once a guru 'worshipped' by thousands, takes the lid off the new movement in his autobiography *Escape into the Light* and was the major contributor to the brilliant video documentary *Gods of the New Age* (Riverside Films, 1984). The adulation of the guru is, he says, equivalent to worship. The Hindu looks to the guru for salvation.

Interviewed on TV, a former follower of Guru Maharishi Mahesh Yogi said, 'I worshipped him. Therefore everything he said or did or thought was right in my eyes.'

When he was deported from the USA Guru Badwan Raj Neesh owned a 100-square-mile ranch in Oregon and a fleet of Rolls Royces. His red-clad followers flock around him by the thousand and call him 'Highest Spiritual Teacher, Lord of the Universe, Honourable Sir, and King'.

The Indian communities called ashrams, where families are broken up, children being separated from their parents, are proliferating in the West. In an interview, English authority on New Age, Caryl Matriciana said, 'The most heartbreaking result of the guru invasion of the West is the damage and harm it brings to the children. . . . Guruism teaches you to die to the voice of conscience.'

Since the East's hot breath was first felt in the West a generation ago, a mass movement has developed. In the mid-90s it preaches, 'One world and one World Leader the Lord Maitreya'. London's Dr. Benjamin Creme is one of its main spokesmen. In the most recent issue of his pulp-tabloid *The Emergence* (published simultaneously in London, Hollywood, Vancouver, Tokyo, Zurich, Brussels, Paris, Munich, Mexico City and Manilla) under the headline 'World Teacher', Creme announces: 'He has been expected for generations by all the major religions. Christians known Him as the Christ, and expect His imminent return. The Jews await Him as the Messiah, the Hindus look for the coming of Krishna; Buddhists expect him as Maitreya Buddha; the Muslims anticipate the Imam Mahdi. The names may be different but they all designate the same One: the World Teacher, whose personal name is Maitreya. He returns now, at the beginning of the Age of Aquarius, as the teacher and guide for those of every religion and those of no religion. . . .'

Levels of awareness of New Age in the West differ. Among Christians reactions are surprisingly naïve and ill-informed. And this despite a plethora of books against New Age written by Christian clergy. Most, sadly, written from the heart rather than the head. Few, very few, have read New Age publications in any depth, or interviewed any but the occasional New Age follower.

Here we are attempting a corrective. Our aim? To correct disinformation, to warn of the true extent and nature of the New Age menace and to suggest the Gospel response.

We are writing, we believe, to enable Christians to be better prepared to encounter a threat to their faith which, in part, will come from outside the Church and, in part, will come in the form of infiltration within the Church. . . .

New Age is multi-faceted and multi-focused. It has many aspects, fronts, faces and phases. Some — holistic medicine, Greenpeace — have much that is good in them, and much else that is not obviously damaging. Gurus are no longer in the front line, though their beliefs are fundamental to everything. Nor is the occult up front in the New Age approach to modern society; as with pornography, there is softcore and hardcore New Age.

A unique set of circumstances has come together to make New Age peculiarly appealing. These circumstances are such that millions of people have been prepared to set aside all that is rational about their nature and accept the unreason of the gurus. The great problem of the *fin de siècle* West is not scientific scepticism but public credulity. People are prepared to believe anything provided that it is communicated with sufficient self-assurance. If it were just a case of simple naïvety it wouldn't be so bad. But behind the gullibility of the modern West lies something more sinister which is at least as much a threat to the educated as it is to the simple.

Through its various fronts, some presenting a verbose, seductive baloney, others appearing to meet felt needs, New Age is luring millions into a shadowy world of terrifying, sanity-destroying, hard-core occult activity. Through its infiltration of Hollywood, the TV companies, the publishing world and the worlds of business and commerce, New Age is gaining a stranglehold over the means by which our views and attitudes are shaped, and our prosperity and employment secured. It is in a position to advance its own ideas and, at the same time, undermine and caricature Christianity. It can interfere with employment and promotion prospects. Benjamin Creme's periodical *The Emergence* makes no secret of the aims of New Age. They want to establish a 'New World Order' which will represent 'one world' under one world leader they identify as Lord Maitreya. New Agers tell us that on the cusp of the centuries the Age of Pisces (Christianity) will give way to the Age of Aquarius (the New Age). This 'paradigm shift', they tell us, will be more radical than either the Renaissance or the Reformation. It will overturn every traditional assumption about life, the nature of reality and the future of the planet. What began with many gurus will end with one great guru — a Guru or Teacher for all religions.

The question is, Are Christians prepared to 'give way' on so fundamental an issue as the religion of Jesus Christ? As century-end approaches can we not find in Christ's Gospel the elements to explode into the greatest revival since Wesley, since Luther, since Paul, since Pentecost?

I have watched New Age grow from the universities of the 60s. Here I tell its story and, in taking it apart, separate what is new in New Age from what is almost as old as time. The writings of the gurus and the superstars are worked over. The developments that have made New Age a mass movement are analysed. The felt needs to which they have given rise are examined.

However, I have endeavoured to occupy as much space unveiling the Gospel solution to the human condition, as to elucidating New Age beliefs — in their essentials, the antithesis of the Gospel of Christ.

The Fine Art of Baloney Detection

Hyde Park Corner on a summer Sunday in 1992. I had an hour to kill before a 'grand opening' I had to cover for my newspaper.

Away from the shouters, but well within sight of Marble Arch, a cross-legged guru sat addressing a motley assortment of 'disciples'. He could have used a short course in voice projection as I only caught snatches of what he said; 'Delve within. . . . Seek your Higher Self. . . . Meditation will lead you into the realm of the spiritual. . . . God is not up there, he's in here' — he thumped his chest — 'God is within you. The whole object of your life is to find him. . . . This is the only reality; Yoga cuts the relationship between the soul and the bodily world. . . . Release the serpent force. . . .'

The next day I was in my dentist's surgery. He was running late. I was having an impacted wisdom tooth removed. Pretending unconcern, I feverishly picked over the magazines on the table. The title of one article hit out at me: 'The Fine Art of Baloney Detection'. The author was sending up gurus in a fashion that, but for the circumstances, might have made me guffaw. After a hundred minutes of torture to which I was subsequently subjected by my friendly dentist, little remained of the article in my memory apart from its title.

Baloney detection is a fine art which we all need to develop these days. Baloney of all types is coming at us from every direction. Clever-sounding baloney. Pious-sounding baloney. Intriguing-sounding baloney. Seductive-sounding baloney. Not to mention the spicy-scented baloney of the East.

Baloney is non-rational. But, sometimes, it sounds so very nearly rational that, unless you know where the baloney artists are coming from, what false assumptions they are building on, you could mistake baloney for sweet reason. Thousands have done this and been drawn into a vortex of horror that has made having a wisdom tooth sawn in half and yanked out of one's jaw seem like an experience to be looked forward to like a picnic.

WANTED. BALONEY DETECTOR. AND/OR YARDSTICK AGAINST WHICH ARGUMENTS CAN BE MEASURED TO DETERMINE WHETHER BALONEY OR TRUTH.

The 60s generation

The 60s generation — especially those involved in higher education in that decade — did not invent baloney. We just generated far more of it than was our fair share. While President Lyndon Johnson made war in Vietnam my generation became peaceniks, beatniks or hippies. We talked about sex as if we'd just invented it. We talked flower power and dressed in a fashion that made our parents call for smelling salts. (Not me, you understand. The nearest I got to fashion *à la mode* was a brown cord jacket. We cultivated a more detached view in the older universities. . . .)

But no sooner had the flower children acquired their BAs and BScs, swapped their VW beetles and Citroen 2cvs for Cortina ghias and BMWs, exchanged their beads for briefcases — and taken time out for a haircut — than they realized that something disturbing was going on. The self-conscious baloney they had talked — *knowing* it was baloney, knowing that *everyone* knew it was baloney — was being taken seriously by the generation after. And, not only taken seriously, taken further than they would ever have dreamt of taking it.

Shuffling about the university cloisters in search of my doctorate in a brown cord jacket and Hush Puppies I saw it all.

Casualties of a sub-culture

The successors of the beatniks and the flower children were generating a whole world of baloney. A baloney culture. And the baloney of the 60s generation was now received wisdom.

At night, making my way across the moss that passed for grass, to the Masters' accommodation, I found myself picking my way over bodies. *Inert* bodies. They were not drunks. Nor were they the permissive society in action. They were stoned, mind-blown, freaked out on something more potent than the contents of any six-pack.

Professor J. P. Kenyon's first encounter with the drug culture as, having descended the worn-stone staircase through the low door, we emerged into the moss-clad quad, was an experience I shall never forget. A large man, his practice had been to hoist miscreants to their feet, having first acquired a strong purchase on their collars with a large right hand. Then he would stuff into their clothing an official-looking piece of paper informing them that, at an unreasonable hour the following morning, they should come up before him and present him, no excuses, with a (usually large) sum of money by way of a fine.

But to hoist these far-outs to their feet was not among the options open to Professor Kenyon. Their eyes, invariably wide open, stared into nothingness, their faces looked like something AWOL from a fishmonger's slab and their bodies were dead weight. It was not long after his first encounter with the drug culture, that he came across one victim who was dead-weight *literally*. . . . And, half a dozen others who, having experienced 'bummers' or 'bad trips' had to be admitted to medical or psychiatric hospitals or special clinics immediately. What appeared to shock him above all was not that this was happening, but that this was happening here, under his nose. In no time he had arranged a transfer to what he believed would be the purer environment of a Scottish university. When, after a short while, the problem had emerged there, he became Professor of History at the University of Kansas — where discipline was the concern of armed police, not Masters of Colleges or Wardens of Halls.

Sea-change in thought

Those of the psychedelic generation who, by being discreet in their drug abuse, managed to avoid being sent down, did a lot of talking. Those who stopped short of drug abuse but had a sneaking regard for those who didn't, did even more. The talking was done in the Buttery, in seminars over which I presided, in junior common rooms and, it must be admitted, sometimes in the senior common rooms to which I now had access as a post graduate. The 'psychedelic generation' had become a loose arrangement, having pulled in not a few dons who aspired to 'stay with' the coming sea-change in thought (and, in a few cases, hoped they were not too old to grab a ticket to the permissive society that seemed to accompany it . . .).

Sometimes the talking led to a more-or-less coherent argument. On a number of occasions the argument spilled over into the debates chamber. Once in that chamber — modelled on the House of Commons — the argument seemed so preposterous that I rose to my feet, exposed a few of its more obvious fallacies and advanced what I called 'the Christian Alternative'.

At the end of that debate everyone seemed to want to exit the debates chamber at the same time. As the crush of bodies squeezed through the arched-over walkways into the streets my Hush Puppies lost contact with the ground. I was lifted from under the armpits for some yards. Then, as the crowd thinned, I was dumped on the cobble-stones. The chap who stood on my torso growled, 'So that's what you think, do you?'

As the crowd-stragglers lurched on down the street they were singing a song made popular by the smash-hit musical *Hair!* 'This is the dawning of the Age of Aquarius. . . .'

The mind-set of the coming generation, I mused, was a deal less tolerant than the 60s lot had been.

And it was, as I recall, no great consolation as I shook

off what I could of the crud-crust that covered the wet cobbles that I was merely a victim of baloney.

The Age of Aquarius

Even when I took my doctorate in the mid-70s and quit the cloisters for the real world I had yet to hear the word now used to describe the new way of thinking.

I use the phrase 'way of thinking' since to call it 'system of thought' would attribute to it a coherence it did not and does not have. And to call it a 'religion' would attribute to it a dignity and uniformity of perception it did not and does not have.

Nevertheless, the main elements of the new way of thinking had, by the mid-70s, become apparent, as had the fact that they were not really new at all.

Hot breath of the East

The hot breath of the East was being felt on Western university campuses in the early 70s. And *off* university campuses too, for that matter. The seductive scents of Eastern religions mixed with the dying embers of the hippy culture and the hedonism of the pop culture, to produce a potent cocktail.

Sometimes I had to pinch myself when, in discussion, I found myself surrounded by Zen Buddhists. At one time, it seemed, I couldn't step out without stubbing my toe on an adherent of Zen.

But Hinduism was there too. And, as far as I am concerned, it came in courtesy of the Beatles, those pied-pipers of the 60s recycled for the 70s with an 'intelligent' image. Their visit in 1969 to the Maharishi Mahesh Yogi's community in India received massive publicity. Soon Transcendental Meditation (TM, for short) was giving 'Beatle mania' a whole new meaning. For millions of Beatles fans on both sides of the Atlantic TM came to be called the 'scientific Yoga'. In no time it had three million followers in the West. TM was, said George Harrison, 'an even more powerful way to bliss consciousness than drugs'.

After the breakup of the 'fab four' George Harrison and John Lennon continued to keep in contact with their gurus. Both were writing lyrics containing the esoteric 'wisdom' of the East. Harrison made Mantra Yoga acceptable through his song 'My Sweet Lord' in which he incorporated the chant to the Hindu god Hare Krishna with the Christian shout of praise 'Hallelujah!' Questioned on the BBC's Sunday 'God Slot', Harrison explained that he was trying to show that Christianity and Hinduism were essentially the same, and to make Hinduism more acceptable.

But within the wake of Mantra Yoga came Sidhi Yoga and Tantra Yoga together with levitation and all manner of occult phenomena. . . .

Soon the London underground was splurged with enormous pictures of less-than-photogenic gurus, atop cryptic messages implying that it was time to consign Christianity to the dustbin of history. Scores of gurus were flying West in search of fame and fortune. During a visit to the United States I caught the hype put out in advance of the arrival of the Guru Magaraj Ji who called himself 'The divine light' and was a man of immense wealth. 'He is coming in the clouds,' read the blurb, 'and with great power and glory. His silver steed will drift down . . . '. After that it got a bit banal: '. . . at 4pm, Los Angeles International Airport, TWA Flight 761.' And when he landed customs officials found his suitcase full of diamonds and other jewels, plus $65,000-worth of undeclared foreign currency. . . .

By now there was almost a conscious search for a name for the new way of thinking. Marilyn Ferguson wrote about it as 'The Movement That Has No Name'. She said, 'It seems to speak of something very old. And perhaps, by integrating magic, science, art and technology, it will succeed where all the king's horses and all the king's men failed.'

By mid-decade it was evident to all that the Age of Aquarius entailed a great deal more than Zen Buddhism with a Western face.

New Age and Eastern religion

With a view to making sense of the thinking of my colleagues — and discovering what they were finding so seductively attractive — I dug out of Senate House library some reliable tomes and gradually got a grip on what they were saying.

Distilled down for convenience, it went:

HINDUISM. Hinduism emerged from the Indus Valley around 1500 BC. The Vedic scriptures it held sacred spiritualized human experience and laid emphasis on the search for 'inner knowledge' and on 'karma' (the 'debt' accumulated against a soul as a result of good or bad actions committed during one's life or lives that determined the form of one's next reincarnation). 'Yoga' meditation was very much a part of the search for 'inner knowledge' or 'enlightenment'.

Hinduism's goal is absorption into the 'absolute'. But on the way to 'the absolute' there were to be many reincarnations (especially essential for those lower down the caste ladder).

For the Hindu, spiritual truth was taught through myth. Most famous was the Bhagavad Gita, the story of Krishna, an incarnation of Vishnu. Many Hindus await the arrival of a golden age via violent global conflict brought on by a final incarnation of Vishnu.

BUDDHISM. Buddhism appeared around 500 BC; the creation of a Hindu prince, Siddhartha Gautama (later called the 'Buddha').

In common with Hinduism, Buddhism lays stress on the search for truth through enlightenment within. The secret of the rapid spread of Buddhism was its ability to adapt itself to the religious and cultural environment of any country where it was propagated. This adaptability is the main reason why Buddhism has been the greatest single influence on what we have called the 'new way of thought'. Its lack of rigidity and the broadness of its concepts made it easy for apologists in the West to give it a face acceptable to the religious and cultural environment of the West.

To the Buddhist, an aspect of the pursuit of enlightenment was the elimination of selfish desires through an eightfold path: righteous belief, aims, speech, conduct, occupation, effort, thinking and meditation. Buddhists worship no gods, believing that their final goal, Nirvana, is achieved without divine assistance. Reached, in fact, through repeated reincarnations, each one the reward for the last. Nirvana is loss of self and freedom from suffering. Built into Buddhism is the belief that it is given to some of their number, like Buddha himself, to be enlighteners of others.

Zen Buddhism has proved most attractive in the West because of its emphasis on self-help salvation; on achieving perfection in this life through personal effort.

New Age: In on the ground

Expressed thus it is puzzling why, in countries like the USA, Britain and Germany where the Christian tradition was strong, Eastern religions should have proved so attractive.

The fact is, of course, that the thought-leaders of the new movement rarely, if ever, mentioned Hinduism or Buddhism. Their method was eclectic. They drew out of the Eastern religions concepts and practices that appealed to them, discarded the rest — and provided no footnotes. It must be understood, too, that just as the much-vaunted sex revolution and leftist leanings of the 60s movement represented self-conscious rebellion against the Christianity of an earlier generation, so the new movement of the 70s represented reaction against a Christian past. It did not seem to matter to the new no-name rebels seduced by the East that it was a Christian past that had never been. That

Christianity had not so much been tried and found wanting, but had never been tried.

On any day of the week you could stop half a hundred shaven-headed Hare Krishna disciples down Oxford Street. If they were too far into their mantra, questions were pointless and conversation impossible; their minds were vacuous. Catch them early and you could learn all about reincarnation or, as they preferred to call it, 'transmigration of the soul'. There was, they told me, no escape from the endless wheel of 'samsara', life and death. In Hinduism, unlike Christianity, there is no forgiveness because there is no sin. I put it to them, 'If there is no forgiveness, there is no hope. . . .' I could see from their faces that it was true.

It was in the spring of 1977 that I first encountered the term New Age movement, and realized then that the witches' cauldron of ideas had acquired a name. The West had its own patent blend of Hinduism and Zen Buddhism camouflaged with psychological terminology.

Research has since yielded the fact that, as early as 1966, an international Hindu conference had laid plans for a sort of Hindu crusade to convert the world. The gurus were chosen as the first crusaders. At the World Congress of Hinduism in 1979 a spokesman declared, 'Our mission in the West has been crowned with fantastic success. Hinduism is becoming the dominant world religion, and the end of Christianity is near.'

Major gatherings of New Agers were organized in the late 70s. The first was organized in London in 1977 by Graham Wilson who gave reincarnation its distinctively Western interpretation; 'Reincarnation is an upward evolution to a higher species of mankind.' Similar festivals followed in European and North American cities. The largest was the Mind, Body, and Spirit festival in Los Angeles. In each of the festivals gurus were involved, TM was taught, all forms of Yoga advocated, together with astrology, palmistry, psychic readings, healings and meditation.

The 80s would produce many in-depth analyses of the

New Age movement. The best took the form of two lengthy documentary-style videos put out by Riverside Films Ltd. in 1984, *Gods of the New Age*. Regrettably the earlier Christian attempts to come to grips with the new movement were not as successful, though there were enough to fill whole bookshelves in Christian book stores.

By the time Ken Wade published his *Secrets of the New Age* (Review and Herald) in 1989, the complexity of the movement was beginning to get through to a Christian readership, but not its menace. Lancashire cleric Kevin Logan talked up the menace aspect in articles in the Christian press. However, when he came to publish his *Close Encounters with the New Age* (Kingsway, 1991) his approach was somewhat muted. He had done a week's course at the New Age training centre in Findhorn on the Moray Firth. Like Wade he highlighted the courtesy and tolerance of New Agers. However, his description of his discussions at Findhorn were such that Stan Stanfield, a member of the Findhorn Foundation, gave Logan's book not only a rave review but a favourable Foreword.

However, on behalf of those of us who were in on the ground when the movement first began to pick up speed in the 70s, I would have to say that 'courtesy' and 'tolerance' were a touch less apparent in those days. Would it be too cynical of me to suggest that 'courtesy' and 'tolerance' are an excellent policy for a movement that, by its own confession, aims to attract enough adherents to replace Christianity by the end of the century?

No New Age publication makes a secret of their belief that Christianity has represented the Age of Pisces (the fish); and that New Age represents the Age of Aquarius, the age to be ushered in on the cusp of the new century.

Similarly no New Ager, except one on the nearest fringe (or one setting out deliberately to deceive), and no New Age publication, would refute the connection that exists, and has existed from the off, between New Age and the occult.

The Occult Connection

The lady at the other end of the line was irate.

She had just read *The Devil Hides Out* (Autumn House, 1991). In it I had laboured the New Age–Occult connection. It was not that she denied this connection. What had made her mad was that, according to her, I had tied New Age in with witchcraft and Satanism.

Well, it was *her* call. And she barely paused for breath anyway. Had she done so I should have told her that the tie-up was made in a quotation from *Christian Weekly* (now absorbed by *The Church of England Newspaper*). And, further, that the author of the article from which the quote was taken had been Robert Runcie, then Archbishop of Canterbury. Not that I have any objection to keeping exalted company. . . .

A curse

Before she rang off she roundly cursed me in the name of somebody I hadn't heard of, and said something about 'spirits' and 'masters'.

Ten days later an accident-free driving record was ruined when I was involved in a multiple pile-up on the A1M a few miles north of the Hatfield tunnel. Although it was dark, driving conditions, otherwise, were ideal. At least two young men had to be cut from their Ford cars. An older man who had written off his Volvo Estate in the rear of my Peugeot was rushed off to hospital with severe angina pains. Of the eight or nine drivers involved two were carried away from the scene horizontally and, of the remainder, only two were deemed fit enough to go home instead of hospital. Praise is due to an all-powerful, all-gracious God that I was one of them, and that the other was the man driving the car immediately in front of me. The medic who examined me expressed surprise that there was no evidence of chest injury caused by the safety belt, whiplash neck caused by the impact, or even any obvious signs of shock.

Then and since, two texts of Scripture have repeatedly come to mind. The first is Numbers 23:23 in which God promises protection for His people against 'sorcery' and 'divination' (NIV). The second is Psalm 34:7, 8 (NIV):

'The angel of the Lord encamps around those who fear him, and he delivers them. . . . Blessed is the man who takes refuge in him.'

The core of New Age

The lady who made the phone call? Her curses had provided proof of the connection made by the Archbishop — and, later, by religious journalist Tony Higton — between New Age and the hard-core occult; the connection she had rung up to deny.

'New Agers can be really nice people. They're into caring and wholeness. And they're close to nature. The term "New Age" conjures up scenes of hills, forests, sunsets, planet earth and other nice images.

'Don't underestimate its attractions. Its occult connections are initially well camouflaged beneath its seductive exterior. *It's actually closely connected with spiritualism, witchcraft and only a short step from Satanism.*' Revd Tony Higton.[1]

New Age has many different *faces* and many different *phases*. Among its *faces* are a number of movements connected with ecology, and a variety of forms of alternative medicine, as well as the more obvious conflation of Eastern religion (adapted to Western tastes) and spiritism. Some who regard themselves as New Agers and are involved in, say, the green movement or acupuncture, would deny all connection between New Age and the occult. They are in the earlier phases of New Age involvement. 'Channelling' and other occult activities will come later.

Basically there are two *phases* of New Age. First, the quasi-humanistic. Second, the occultic. Many 'humanistic'

New Age fronts appear innocuous enough. But the lady on the other end of the telephone line had progressed from humanism well into the hard-core occult. She was betrayed by her own curses! (Though the supernatural power invoked by her curses proved less than effective in the face of the protection of an all-loving, all-powerful God.)

Exactly how progression from humanism to occultism can happen was well illustrated in the story line of ITV's prime-time New Age drama 'Forever Green', with John Alderton and Pauline Collins. A plot that began in preoccupation with clean country living, 'green' concerns and humanistic wisdom, rolled into *shia-tsu*, and from there to ghosts, channelling and even 'spirit-writing'. Perhaps *shia-tsu*, considered by the rich and famous as a trendy form of 'alternative medicine', had been the bridge.

Yoga

In the West, Yoga was once the preserve of a microminority of occultists. Now nineteen million Americans practise it and millions more in Europe.

New Age has made reincarnation a trendy belief with a positive connotation in the West. In the East, without question, it is a punishment. In the Hindu religion the only way of escape from the endless cycle of living and dying is through Yoga.

In the West, Yoga is marketed rather differently.

Mantra Yoga involves breathing and meditation exercises aimed at 'dissolving the mind'. The *mantra* is the name of a Hindu god endlessly repeated until the mind is cleared of all thought. A variant of this was used as a brainwashing technique in the totalitarian regimes before the end of the Cold War.

Raja Yoga has been called 'the highest form of Hinduism'. *Raj* means 'royal'. This intense form of meditation is also aimed at emptying the mind. But further than that, the aim is to 'connect with the Supreme Being'. This is the means of spirit possession.

Tantra Yoga is, at present, spreading like a forest fire

through Western countries. Like all Yoga it is designed to provoke possession by Hindu spirits in order to break the chain of reincarnation. However, Tantra is practised by 'advanced' disciples and brings the psychic powers to full bloom. It has had horrifying results from degenerate behaviour to satanic practices and murder.

All forms of Yoga suspend the reasoning powers, empty the mind and enable spirits to possess it. Some years ago, at the Frankfurt Book Fair, I interviewed Johanna Michaelsen, author of *The Beautiful Side of Evil* (Harvest House) and a former Yoga teacher. Johanna, now a Christian, said, 'The purpose of the meditations in all forms of Yoga is to make the mind blank. This is terribly dangerous. It's like opening the door to a room. Whatever comes through, you have no control over.'

The great deception with regard to Yoga is that nowadays it is invariably marketed as physical exercise — no more. No mention is made of Hinduism or of the significance of the words chanted in the mantras.

Yoga is the transition between the humanistic and occult phases of New Age for most of those who become involved.

An occult happening

My first brush with the occult phase of New Age happened about the time *Hair* hit the West End. In the university Buttery I had been involved in an evening discussion with an assortment of Zen Buddhists, TM practitioners and 'Theol' undergraduates. It was then fashionable among the university Theology fraternity to define God in terms first coined by John Robinson, then Bishop of Woolwich, in *Honest To God* — 'the ground of our being', 'the deep-down in everyone's consciousness'; terms now very much a part of New Age jargon.

When I left to turn in for the night the discussion was still going good.

Some time later I was awakened to hear a rowdy crowd of undergraduates crossing the landing and entering the room next to mine. They settled down quickly. Soon a sonorous chant penetrated the stout wall. It was the sound 'Om' in endless repetition. My neighbours, I knew, were chanting a *mantra* in an attempt to empty the mind and achieve what they had told me was 'cosmic consciousness' (oneness with the universe and 'god', though not with the God of the Judaeo-Christian tradition). 'Om' was a word symbolizing the god Brahma.

I woke up around 2am to hear hell breaking loose next door. It sounded as if the stout furniture provided by the university authorities was being flung around the room. There were hysterical screams. My heart collided rather violently with my front teeth. Donning my dressing-gown I opened my door in time to see the neighbouring door fall in with a bang that had the report of a cannon and awoke the whole quad. Students — my discussion companions of the previous evening — came scrambling out, ashen pale, stumbling over one another in their eagerness to put space between themselves and that room. Last to leave, dazed and weeping, was the fellow post-graduate whose room it was. He never returned to it again.

It was lunch the following day before I caught up with any members of the group who had caused such a commotion the previous night. I found half a dozen of them crouched over a mahogany table in one of the city's ancient eating places. They could hardly have looked worse had they been in the final stages of terminal cancer. Eleven hours after the events in the room next to mine, two of them were still shaking. Sucking desperately on their cigarettes, over meals they did not get round to eating, they cautiously answered my questions.

Findhorn, TM and Channelling

What had been going on in the room next to mine had been more than transcendental meditation. One member of the group, during the long summer vacation, had joined the Findhorn Community on the Moray Firth in Scotland. Here he had learned that TM was merely the preliminary exercise in 'channelling'. In the evolutionary scheme of things, so he had been taught, some humans had evolved to a state far in advance of others. This elite of 'enlightened ones' enjoyed certain advantages over others, including psychic abilities. Living 'enlightened ones' could act as channellers (mediums) for 'enlightened ones' (masters or christs) who had 'passed over to the other side'.

The previous night they had sought to put the Findhorn channelling procedure into practice. By the use of a mantra they had sought completely to empty their minds, to render them 'vacant possession'. By doing this, they had been told, one, some, or possibly all of them, might experience spirit possession and begin to channel the wisdom of some dead master. The curious thing about the midnight meeting was that the 'dead master' they had sought to channel was the Apostle Paul, author of the greater part of the New Testament!

Over their cold lunches I was told that they had not known exactly what to expect. Would it be an alien voice speaking through them? Or would ectoplasm (which usually manifests itself as a filmy substance pouring from a medium's bodily openings and supposedly denoting the presence of a disembodied spirit) emerge, as in a 'conventional' spiritist seance?

Something heavy going down

In the event, after a prolonged period of chanting their mantra, each member of the group, in turn, had begun to experience nervousness, a feeling of profound depression — and a feeling that 'something really heavy was going down'. Some had confessed later that Ultimate Evil was present in the room. Among those who had felt this had been the post-graduate whose room it was. What had brought the channelling session to such a dramatic conclusion had been the fact that, simultaneously, certain members of the group had experienced blows to the head and items of furniture had begun to move (all without human assistance).

The conclusion of the session had been brought about

when 'something' had appeared in the room (no one was able to describe what it was), and the door of its own volition had suddenly fallen in. 'The rest you know,' I was told.

Needless to say, the Apostle Paul had *not* put in an appearance!

While by no means a typical channelling session, this had, without question, been an occult manifestation. Some of those who had witnessed it I did not see again; our paths never crossed. Others, including the half dozen I met in the eating house, kept New Age and the occult at arm's length from that day forth. However, at least two members of the group lived to recover their nerve. Indeed, they became known as 'the gurus', only partly in jest. Certainly they always had a ready audience for their words. It was clear that, in some sense, they enjoyed a sense of power as a result of their brush with the supernatural.

---

[1]Tony Higton, 'The New Age Meets its Match', *Christian Weekly*, 29 June 1990, page 6 (italics ours).

The Age of Unreason

By the end of the 70s all manner of air-headed nonsense was being talked and written in the name of New Age.

And not only in the world of academe.

New Age had broken loose and its jargon was parroted in the staff-rooms of reputable comprehensives, over coffee by 'young executives' in fashionable cafes, on TV talk shows — and by the black briefcase brigade on the 8.14 to Euston. It was difficult to talk through a problem without someone chipping in with a comment like, 'There's a Force that says all this was meant to be,' or 'Look into the deep resources of the inner-self and you will know that "right" and "good" are without meaning. . . .'

It often struck me that the world was relapsing into rain-dancing when everyone knew the answer lay in irrigation. We were entering an age of unreason in which baloney was spoken unchallenged by the most surprising of people.

Celebrities climb aboard

British Royals were dabbling in forms of alternative medicine which, a generation before, would have been bracketed with witchery.

Hollywood stars (like the characters they played on screen) were increasingly preoccupied with their karma. Some had found a lucrative sideline in writing books of esoteric 'wisdom' in which they revealed who they had been in previous reincarnations. Shirley MacLaine, with thirty-four movies to her credit, was also claiming to have been astrally projected beyond the Earth's atmosphere and to have looked down on us all (including herself), unsure whether she would ever return again. She was making millions from her New Age TV series and from books with titles like *Out on a Limb, You can get there from here*, *Going Within* and *Dancing in the Light*, all complete with tales of channelling the spirits of the long-since dead.

'You have to deal with your own inner self,' wrote the star of *Sweet Charity*. 'Often you find HS.' Ms MacLaine was not thinking about the Holy Spirit, but 'the Higher Self'. In the same book there were multiple references to the 'HS' speaking to her; and, from the content of the messages communicated, it was clear that the 'voice' involved was that of a far-from-holy spirit. 'You each have to deal with your inner self, and your inner self reveals that *you* are god. Every other person is god also. Each needs to become master of his own soul; which is to say, to realize he is god. The god energy is no judge of persons; there *is* no judgement. There is only one experience. Incarnation after incarnation until the soul realizes its perfection, and that is total love.' *Dancing in the Light*, page 340.

Shirley's HS told her there was no difference between right and wrong (page 342). Every inner self was god, enlightenment being paced according to individual requirements, carnal and extraterrestrial. 'We are our own creators' (page 343). Evil and good did not exist; only 'enlightened awareness or ignorance' (page 347).

'Previous incarnations'

The parts of Shirley MacLaine's self-revelation that snatched the attention of the TV talk show hosts and the tabloid editors were those with regard to her previous reincarnations (pages 354, *et seq.*), and with regard to the occult (pages 366, *et seq.*). Shirley had, apparently, seen herself with a herd of elephants in the bush jungles of India in one previous existence. Her Higher Self had identified her name as Asana. She had been known as the Princess of the Elephants. (In more recent years Ms MacLaine has revealed a few of her other reincarnations; invariably, like others who ply her trade, identifying with the great and the good of previous centuries, never with the lower social orders. . . .) She had seen herself dancing in a harem, as a Spanish infanta wearing diamond earrings, as a monk meditating in a cave, as an infant lifted by an eagle and deposited with a primitive family in Africa, as a ballet dancer in Russia, as a Japanese princess in a brightly-coloured kimono.

L. Ron Hubbard and Scientology

By now the bandwagon was rolling. One who had given it an initial shove and was now rolling with it to unprecedented success was the founder of Scientology, L. Ron Hubbard. Hubbard had been integrating Eastern religion with Western pseudo-science since the 50s. Now he could not believe his good luck. His particular form of unreason had become a fad. Scientology was no longer marginalized but was part of a movement that seemed to be the *Zeitgeist* of the age. Suddenly Scientology centres were springing up all over the place and steady queues of the credulous were forming to have their personalities 'audited'. By the early 80s Scientology was claiming more supporters than the Jehovah's Witnesses and the Mormons combined, and L. Ron Hubbard's books were reaching the best-seller ratings.

Hubbard's whole life fed on fantasy. Many of his books had not been written as fiction. Nevertheless they were all sold under 'fiction' in the bookshops. Hubbard had always declared himself 'a nuclear physicist' (despite the fact that he had failed at every school he ever attended).

Recruits to Scientology are typically young, intelligent and idealistic. In a very short time they become fanatics, impervious to reason and quick to cut themselves off from anyone who wants to apply reason to their cherished baloney. Young people are instructed by their Scientology organizations to 'disconnect' from their families. 'Disconnect' means exactly that: sever all relations. Such estrangements are invariably deep and lasting, leaving heart-sick parents no longer able to speak in any way to their children, and certainly not rationally.

Governments against Scientology

Nabraska-born Hubbard published his first best-seller *Dianetics: the Modern Science of Mental Health* in 1950. His first brush with the authorities came in 1963 when agents of the Food and Drug Administration raided Scientology's Washington headquarters and seized a number of E-meters (the lie-detectors used by Scientology students in 'auditing' personalities, an extremely crude and dangerous form of psycho-analysis which in many instances has led to disastrous consequences). Shortly afterwards the Australian government put out a multi-page document explaining that Scientology was a great danger to everyone who became involved with it and that its founder was 'pathologically deficient'. The British government hounded Hubbard from his hideaway in a Sussex mansion. For years he was hunted by the US government while he roamed the world's oceans — beyond government control — on a flotilla of ships.

Hubbard was 'at sea', on the run from the governments of three major Western nations, *before* Scientology became a mass movement. The immense and well-documented case against this fugitive from justice contains acres of facts that have to be ignored, put aside, by the millions who have joined the Scientology movement. But it is in the nature of unreason to push aside facts. The young idealists who continue to flock to the movement still believe that they are maximizing their human potential, becoming better people. L. Ron Hubbard's thoroughly-discredited pseudo-science of mental health, Dianetics, gained rather than lost currency during the 80s. The highest sales of Hubbard's books have been grossed since his death in 1985 and have never been greater than at present. Those who embark on the Scientology odyssey are seeking freedom from guilt and 'engrams' (personality problems), and are pursuing 'clear' (perfection).

Scientology's view of Jesus Christ is typical of that of other New Age cults. Hubbard declared that Jesus Christ was more or less free of 'engrams' and that his personality was 'just above clear'. 'Just above clear', but significantly lower than that of L. Ron Hubbard. . . .

New Age on TV

An interesting insight into the pseudo-intellectual 'unreason' of the New Age movement — as of its hold over the media — was given in a series of five fifty-minute TV programmes put out by Britain's commercial Channel 4 on Sunday evenings in the winter of 1991. The format of each programme was the same: an articulate, photogenic New Age interviewer with a studio audience of between thirty and forty New Age 'intellectuals'. The general impression of the debate was rather like that given by New Age music: soothing, bland and benign.

A viewer with no background in New Age observation was in dire need of a baloney detector — and a dictionary! The dictionary, however, would have had to have been a special New Age edition since a high proportion of the words employed were not to be found in either *Webster's* or the *Concise Oxford*. But it all sounded very profound. Bland, sweeping statements that were both tediously obvious and false at the same time. There was the usual mix of religion and philosophy but, perhaps, a de-emphasis on the occult aspects. Nevertheless the overall impression was the one that New Age always gives, that Jungian psychology is being mixed up with palmistry and tarot cards; that the jargon of Hinduism and Buddhism is being boiled up with the virtues of veganism and the ideology of Greenpeace. One critic suggested an alternative title for the series: *How to Reach Nirvana Using Garlic*.

Damage to the green movement

Nevertheless the series was not without its dangers. This was especially evident when environmental issues were being discussed. When genuine scientific concerns with regard to earth-warming, the ozone layer, the depletion of the rain forests and the pollution of the seas, are put side by side with talk of biorhythms, ley-lines and re-incarnation, it robs the whole debate of credibility. It is harder to convince politicians that the green debate is more than a passing fad when TV exponents of it are would-be descendants of Egyptian sun gods who are telling a mass audience that 'the Earth is our mother and we have behaved badly to her, so now she is punishing us . . . '. The British Green Party lost its credibility and the heavyweights withdrew their support from it because of the New Age connection.[1]

The same applies to the diet debate. The nutritional revolution of the 70s and 80s has provided conclusive proof that it is *not* a good idea to live on a diet of high fat cheese, cholesterol-heavy burgers and chips fried in finest Brent crude. But who is going to listen to those arguments when they are mixed up with talk about karma and the importance of balancing your yin and yang?

Commenting on the fact that at least 1,000 channellers were practising in Los Angeles alone and that channelling was 'old Spiritualism recycled' Brooks Alexander wrote: 'There is irony in the fact that this spiritual relic is the latest rage of our "secular" age, the hottest fad of the so-called New Age movement.[2] Another authority has it; 'The New Age movement seems to be a reaction to the scientific age. During a time when everything has become so objective and particularized, the shift now is to emphasize the subjective and the whole (holistic).[3]

By the early 80s, whether they knew it or not, most people in Western nations had heard New Age ideas, listened to New Age music, viewed New Age art, watched New Age superstars — perhaps even read New Age literature and bought New Age products. But the face of New Age in which a majority of the population was actually involved was part of its 'occult' rather than 'humanistic' phase.

Astrology had upwards of one billion followers world-wide.

[1]*The Sunday Times*, 30 August 1992, News Review, page 5. [2]Brooks Alexander, 'Theology from the Twilight Zone', *Christianity Today*, 18 September 1987, page 25. [3]J. H. Berry, *New Age Movement* (BTB 1988), page 8.

Your Fate in the Stars?

'I don't believe in all this astrology nonsense. We Virgos are not so easily taken in. . . .'

I can't guarantee that anyone actually said that. But the joke has certainly done the rounds. Its popularity may be because it typifies the ambivalent view of the Western sophisticate to the essentially Eastern occult form cum pseudo science of astrology.

The surveys that ascertained the actual extent of astrology's hold on Western nations were conducted following the publication of Joan Quigley's *What Does Joan Say?* after the 1980-88 Reagan presidency.

Quigley, it will be recalled, had been Nancy Reagan's astrologer. And the book was an account of the Reagan presidency that came out of Nancy's daily telephone consultations with her.

Many, myself included, laughed at Quigley's revelations at first. After all, she *did* make it sound as if she was all but running the planet during the eight-year presidency. She certainly took credit for the nuclear weapons deal that 'Ronnie' reached with Gorbachev; 'Ronnie's Mercury was very close to Gorbachev's Venus,' she said by way of explanation and, what's more, 'both were in Capricorn on the first occasion they met. . . .'

According to Ms. Quigley, she enabled 'Ronnie' to win his pre-election presidential debates by picking the most propitious time for them. She also claimed to have chosen the date for his major cancer operation which, it will be recalled, was successful. Indeed, Nancy's astrologer came close to claiming full credit for ushering in 'a new era of world peace; the New World Order'. A doubtful self-accolade, as George Bush discovered after making the same claim himself following the successful conclusion of the Gulf War. 'New World Order' is New Age jargon; the aim of the whole movement. Quigley knew this when she used the phrase. Did Bush?

Back to Quigley on Reagan. 'Astrology', wrote Quigley, 'assured that nothing unfavourable would "stick" to the President. . . . I was the Teflon in what came to be known as the Teflon Presidency. . . .'

There was not a thing, she said, she could have done about the Iran-Contra Scandal. It seems that in November 1986 Uranus and Saturn had simultaneously entered Ron's horoscope and, once those two rascals are on your case, you might as well pack it in and go to bed.

During the Reagan presidency, cynical journalists often asked, 'Who's pulling his strings?' Few dreamt it was a psychic. An interesting scenario: the leader of the free world — with one hand on the nuclear button and the other on a crystal ball. Is it a scenario we can take seriously?

What's all the fuss about?

Astrology's baloney-content is quite high.

But is there something beneath the baloney? A power, force, whatever, using astrology to manipulate lives? The same occult force, perhaps, that manifested itself and so completely terrified the assortment of Zen followers and Theology students in the room next to mine?

Those actually involved in astrology take it very seriously. And let's be clear: Today there are more professional astrologers casting horoscopes than there are professional astronomers using telescopes.

Robert Currie, a former stock broker, now runs Equinox, an astrology shop on a chic, pedestrianized alley-way in Covent Garden. He estimates that in ten years as an astrologer he has produced 70,000 personal charts. Each one, sealed in an expensive-looking gold and blue plastic bag, contains two documents of twenty pages each, that look like market-research reports or time-and-motion studies. Showbiz stars and politicians are among Currie's better-known clients. 'The Reagans are by no means an isolated case,' he says. 'The Equinox list is also said to include several members of various royal families. . . . The British Royals are very keen on astrologers. Diana has consulted at least three, including Penny Thornton and Felix Lyle. . . . Princess Margaret has regular consultations. . . . The first newspaper horoscope in the world was printed following the birth of Princess Margaret in August 1930.'[1]

But about the *influence* of astrology, say, on the Reagan presidency. Can we believe Quigley's sweeping claims to influence? Here's what the White House Chief of Staff has written; 'Virtually every major move and decision the Reagans made' was based on the astrological advice of Joan Quigley.[2] The much-publicized dependence of the Reagans on astrology led to a massive increase in its popularity, already considerable. 'Astrologers . . . have hailed the acceptance of astrology at the highest levels of government in one of the most powerful nations on earth as confirmation of its legitimacy.'[3] Nor was Reagan the only head of state to be influenced by astrology.[4]

Astrology has been around for upwards of 3,000 years. However, its practice grew colossally in the 1960s and 70s. And, partly by way of reaction to our increasingly mechanistic and materialistic society, partly following role models like the Reagans, and partly as one aspect of New Age becoming a mass movement, it has never had more adherents than now. Upwards of one billion, world-wide, believe in astrology in some form. It has thirty-two million followers in the USA, *including 10 per cent of all evangelical Christians*. And the ubiquity of astrology columns in newspapers and magazines, the mass sales of astrology books, astrological computer calculators, chart vending machines and assorted trinkets attest to the existence of a vast following among the allegedly hard-headed Western Europeans.[5] 'The stars and the Royals are the twin pillars that hold up half of Fleet Street. Horoscopes help to sell millions of newspapers and magazines.'

Media astrologers, like Patrick Walker and Russell Grant, have made vast fortunes out of the game.[1]

How does it work?

Charles Strohmer was a practising astrologer in the late 1960s and early 1970s.[6] 'Fifty or sixty years ago there was little need to have a manageable understanding of the religion-science of astrology,' he writes. 'It was rare to meet those who took the craft seriously. Today that has changed . . . , *astrology is the leading practice of the so-called New Age movement.*'[7]

What follows is a simplification of the explanation given by astrologers of how their 'craft' works. . . .

For millennia people have traced the outlines of exotic creatures in the patterns formed by the stars. These patterns (or 'constellations') were given the names of mythical figures, like Orion (the Hunter), Ursus Major (the Great Bear), and Pegasus (the Winged Horse). All in all, some eighty-eight constellations were named.

Ancient astronomers noticed, however, that the track of the sun's path through the sky (astronomers call this 'the Zodiac') seemed to pass through twelve of these constellations. These twelve 'signs of the Zodiac' took on a special significance because of that fact.

In time godlike powers were attributed to each of these twelve signs. People came to believe that the stars actually controlled their destinies. 'Individual wills', ancient astrologers said, 'are pushed and pulled by heavenly bodies no less than are the tides. Our fates are written in the stars.'

The client's name, place and date of birth are all an astrologer needs to put together a horoscope. But astrological books are made to sound very scientific. Nevertheless, as Strohmer discovered, it was not the *planets* astrologers were interpreting. It was *the gods they were named after*. To Saturn, Mercury, Venus, Mars, Jupiter and the rest were attributed the characteristics of mythical Greek or Roman deities. Hence, once the astrologer has used the pseudo-scientific information to locate the planets and construct his chart, his studies bear down upon the gods. The 'aspects' (angles) are geometric relationships between the planets (gods), and are believed to have different meanings: adverse, favourable, neutral. The twelve 'houses' are thought to govern different departments of life, for example, finances, family, relationships, etc.

Based on bad astronomy

Astrology is based on bad astronomy. No constellation is actually where astrologers say it is — not even the signs of the Zodiac! As the earth spins on its axis, it wobbles slightly. Granted, it's not much of a wobble, but given the 1,800 years since astrologers last updated their astronomy (astrology is based on Ptolemy's system worked out in the second century AD), it's been more than enough to throw off all their calculations.

The fact of 'wobble' ('precession') means that the constellations shift a little bit to the east each day. Over time, this shift has been enough to move back the ascendance of each sign of the Zodiac by one full month. If your horoscope says you're a Gemini, in other words, you're really a Taurus; if it says you're sign is Libra, it's really Virgo!

If that isn't bad enough, the earth's 'wobble' has skewed the Zodiac enough that it now includes an additional constellation. There are no longer twelve signs of the Zodiac, in other words, but thirteen. You'll search your newspaper's horoscope column in vain before you find any advice for people born under the sign of Ophiuchus (the Serpent-bearer)!

The fact that astrology is bad science could be excused, perhaps, if it gave good advice. Does it?

One physicist checked the birth dates of thousands of scientists and politicians listed in *Who's Who*. According to astrology, after all, those born under certain signs are more likely to enter science and politics. What he found was that their astrological signs were as randomly distributed as those of the general public.

A psychologist at Michigan State University obtained the records of hundreds of couples who had been married and divorced. He discovered that those born under 'compatible' signs married — and divorced — just as often as those under 'incompatible' signs.

A French statistician examined the Zodiac signs, moon signs, planet signs and ascendent signs of over 15,000 successful professionals. The result? The correlation between profession and astrological influence was no better than random chance.

Random chance is really the key to *most* horoscopes. Most of the personality profiles given by them are so general there's a good chance most people will see something of themselves in them. The French statistician just mentioned placed a newspaper ad offering free, personalized horoscopes. One hundred and fifty people responded. After sending each respondent exactly the same information, he asked how well the description fitted. Ninety-four per cent said they recognized themselves — *ninety-four per cent of the people who'd received the horoscope of a mass murderer!*

The baloney content of astrology *is* very high!

So why do so many take it so seriously?

Does it work?

In reply to criticisms most of those who believe their fate is determined by 'the stars' say simply, 'It works'. Does it?

Ex-astrologer Charles Strohmer makes a distinction between the 'charlatans' who write for magazines and tabloid newspapers and 'committed astrologers'. For a number of years he himself was in the latter category. On a number of occasions, he asserts, correct 'self-disclosures' resulted from his interpretation of the charts, it being understood that 'self-disclosure' means information about an individual and his/her past. 'For the astrologer, a confirmation of a self-disclosure is an impressive moment.'[8] It is also an important moment for the client. It is at this point that the client 'begins to believe'. And, having heard a more-or-less accurate 'self-disclosure' the individual will be in a frame of mind to accept the astrologer's forecast of his/her future. Here Strohmer is firm: *Astrologers cannot predict the future.*

So how does 'self-disclosure' work?

The astrologer's mind, says Strohmer, is focused on a portion of the chart he/she believes pertains to a detail in the client's life. The chart, like the palm of a hand or a crystal, can be, he says, the 'contact material' between a psychic and his 'familiar spirit'.

Having spent years studying the workings of astrology, Strohmer is emphatic that correct self-disclosures result from information passed to the astrologer by deceptive 'spirit guides'. He believes these 'spirit guides' to be 'the spirits of devils working miracles'; angels-cum-demons expelled from heaven with Satan before the dawn of earth-history (Revelation 12:7-9; 16:13, 14).

Astrology and the Bible

Astrology is rejected in the Bible because 1. it is futile and worthless; 2. it constitutes involvement with occult powers; 3. it is a form of idolatry (exchanging the heavens for God). 'Astrology is seen to have no power to save men from their sins, instead it opens men to demonic deception.'[9]

The Bible's long list of condemnations of astrology (and pagan gods and practices associated with astrology) is, to say the least, impressive.[10]

The Bible view of the source from which 'genuine' astrologers receive their information — angels-cum-demons[11] — accounts for both the weaknesses and the strengths of astrology. Demons know the past and can throw up a competent self-disclosure for the present; but of the future they know little or nothing. When astrologers descend into specifics — make *specific* predictions — they are wrong 95 per cent of the time! This, at all events, was the upshot of an exhaustive survey of specific predictions made by astrologers over a period of years undertaken by Ralph Blodgett and published in trendy American magazine *Vibrant Life.*[12]

Where's the harm in it? Charles Strohmer speaks from experience; The partnership between the spirit and the spokesperson, he argues, is tremendously damaging to the latter. ' "Channelling" is the foreplay of a deeper intercourse with these spirits: possession. Yet no matter what the degree of involvement, intimacy with the deceptive beings brings about the deterioration of anyone who remains in counsel with them. . . . These spirits will draw him down into their totally depraved state.'[13]

The danger for 'the client'? Because of the forces behind it, astrology leads in the opposite direction from Christianity and in the same direction as witchcraft, spiritism, magic, sorcery and Satanism.[14]

Last days of Hitler

So Ron and Nancy were playing a dangerous game. The same game, in fact, played by Adolf Hitler. One whole wall of Hitler's bunker was taken up with an astrological chart. He and other Nazi leaders were firm believers in astrology. Hugh Trevor Roper in his *Last Days of Hitler*[15] describes how the Nazis received the death of President F. D. Roosevelt. Leading propagandist Josef Goebbels phoned Hitler on his private line; 'My Fuhrer, I congratulate you! Roosevelt is dead! It's written in the stars that the second half of April will be the turning point for us. This is Friday 13 April. It is the turning point.'

It was 1945, and the Red Army was only miles from the Chancellery Building. But Hitler was in ecstasy. Goebbels and Heinrich Himmler were putting all their faith in astrology. Years before, with Hitler, they had drawn up complex astrological charts. And they were still putting their faith in them. It would appear that one of the reasons Hitler kept on when everything was hopeless was his belief in the destiny of Nazism as mapped out in the astrological charts. So many things that had 'appeared in the stars' had taken place. There was still, Goebbels was sure, a 'glorious destiny' ahead; it was all there in the charts.

The lies sustained Hitler until his suicide. But his foul, occult-inspired dreams did not die with him. Others dream on, and their dreams are the world's nightmares.

We may laugh, indulgently, at the eccentricities of the Reagans. But they were playing with dark forces.

[1]*The Sunday Telegraph*, Review section, 23 August 1992. [2]Donald T. Regan, *For the Record: From Wall Street to Washington* (1988), page 3. [3]R. B. Culver, *Astrology: True or False — a Scientific Evaluation* (1988), page ix. [4]John Ankerberg and John Weldon, *Astrology* (1989) page 12. [5]*National and International Religion Report* (4 July 1988), page 1; Lawrence Jerome, *Astrology Disproved* (1975), page 1; J. Ankerberg and J. Weldon, op cit, pages 11, 12; C. Strohmer, *What Your Horoscope Doesn't Tell You* (1988), pages 1-3; Gallup Poll cited *Signs of the Times* (USA), May 1990, page 18. [6]C. Strohmer, op cit, pages 2, 3. [7]Ibid, page 9. [8]Ibid, page 52. [9]J. Ankerberg and J. Weldon, op cit, pages 132-134.[10]Leviticus 18:21; 20:1-6; Deuteronomy 4:19; 17:2-5; 18:9-11; 2 Kings 17:16; 21:3-6; 23:4, 5, 24; Jeremiah 7:18; 8:1, 2; 19:13; Ezekiel 8:10, 11, 16; Amos 5:25, 26; Zephaniah 1:4-6; Acts 7:42; 1 Corinthians 10:20; Galatians 5:19-21; Colossians 2:8, 20; Ephesians 6:10-18. [11]Revelation 12:7-9. [12]*Vibrant Life*, July/August 1986, pages 14-19. [13]Charles Strohmer, op cit, page 71. [14]J. Ankerberg and J. Weldon, op cit, pages 132-164; C. Strohmer, op cit, pages 72-109. [15]Hugh Trevor Roper, *Last Days of Hitler*, page 100.

The American Connection

If astrology involves dabbling with dark forces, Americans, in particular, have something to worry about.

New Age — occult involvement in US

It was between 1978 and 1984 that New Age became a mass movement in the USA. A poll conducted by Gallup found that in 1978 40 per cent of Americans were involved in astrology. A Gallup survey conducted in 1984 found that the percentage involvement had risen to 59.[1]

Recent surveys conducted by Gallup and Northern Illinois University demonstrate the extent to which other concepts and practices central to New Age have caught on in the USA. In 1989 42 per cent of Americans claimed to have been in contact with someone who had died (an increase of 27 per cent from when the poll was taken in 1978). Sixty-seven per cent of all adult Americans (seventy million people) reported having had psychic experiences. A recent survey indicated that 58 per cent of Americans polled believed in reincarnation and that 60 per cent had incorporated *some* aspect of Eastern religion into their world-view. Thirty-four million Americans are concerned with 'inner growth' in the New Age sense. Fourteen per cent of the US population endorsed the work of spiritist mediums and New Age channellers. About half of the American population think extraterrestrial beings have visited Earth. Two thousand YMCAs across America offer Yoga classes and 'nearly two-thirds of all universities and colleges make Yoga available as part of the curriculum'.[2] Another serious survey of the New Age movement in America estimates its following as 'probably more than sixty million, about one-fourth of the population'.[3]

Who would have thought that the no-name movement I watched come together from British universities in the

60s and early 70s would, as New Age, rise to such influence in the world's leading industrialized nation?

In *fin de siècle* USA, New Age is moving to a crescendo. The media swarm to film and televise accounts of trance-channelling (spirit mediumship), healing with crystals, meditation techniques, levitation, psychic surgery and UFO sightings.

New Age and Hollywood

Whether Hollywood has led public attitudes towards New Age or vice versa is a subject for debate. Certainly New Age concepts, jargon, phenomena and concerns have been central to the output of Hollywood since the mid-70s.

To mention *specific* examples of New Age-influenced movies is to invite ridicule. Ordinary people, among them millions of Christians, have viewed these movies either in the cinemas or as videos in the home and have seen nothing wrong with them. Because they were unaware of the New Age connection when they viewed the movie, they refuse to accept that it exists. They have been so used to evaluating the acceptability of movies in terms of sex content, that they have become blinded to obvious symptoms of the influence of Ultimate Evil. Walter Martin, author of *The New Age Cult* (1989), and Dave Hunt, one of America's best known critics of New Age, analysed a whole sequence of movies for New Age content. Among those in which they found New Age (Hindu) influence to be particularly strong were *Close Encounters, Poltergeist, Ghostbusters 1* and *2, ET, Indiana Jones and the Temple of Doom, Return of the Jedi, Gandhi, 2001,* and *Star Wars*. Since the most recent of those movies is now ten years old the likelihood is that Martin and Hunt's research needs updating.

Tal Brooke in *The Cosmic Circuit* considers the Hollywood connection a chief channel for 'vigorously injecting Eastern mysticism into American culture'. He believes that the film *The Last Temptation of Christ* was an attempt to peddle the New Age view of Jesus. Jesus comes over as a fundamentally good Man but with propensities for sinfulness (a sinful nature). 'Everything is a part of God,' declares the tormented Christ.

Douglas Groothuis, an expert on the effects of occult involvement, provides impressive documentation to prove that Charles Manson was 'deeply immersed in the one-for-all' (New Age) movement when he ordered the murders of actress Sharon Tate and several others. 'Manson felt he had reached the state of consciousness beyond morality; therefore, he was free to kill.'[4] Dr. Kenneth Wade's second book on the New Age has as its thesis that, because the movement is an outgrowth of Eastern and other primal religions, and because those religions place a low value on human life, the lasting contribution of New Age to Western culture is likely to be a substantial erosion of the reverence for human life and the provision of rationalizations for murder. Wade cites instances in which the New Age mind-set and specific (occasionally mass) murders are definitely connected.[5]

Spirit guides are not only associated with way out intellectuals or the psychologically unstable. Shirley MacLaine is only the most prominent among superstars claiming that her life, thought and work are directed by the spirits. Linda Evans of *Dynasty*, and Joyce De Witt, formerly of *Three's Company* follow guidance from a spirit entity called Mafu. Other American superstars with strong New Age connections include actresses Sharon Gless and Marsha Mason, singers Helen Reddy and Tina Turner, musician Paul Horn and entertainer Lisa Bonet. New Agers in music and the arts have been slower to go public. However, since eminent British violinist Sir Yehudi Menuhin declared that New Age had a far higher priority in his life even than music, New Age composers, conductors and instrumentalists have been crawling out of the woodwork on all sides.

New Age in the classroom

There is much concern about New Age influence in

the educational system. *Confluent Education* by New Age educationalist Beverley Galyean is widely used in American public schools. The implicit theology of this volume is very interesting to Christians. It leads children to the belief that they are both perfect and divine and that, therefore, the sin problem does not exist and there was no need for Christ or Calvary. Illustrating the impact of New Age on American education Walter Martin says, 'In a Los Angeles public schoolroom twenty-five first-graders lie still as their teacher tells them to imagine they are perfect beings who are full of light and who contain all of the wisdom of the universe within them.'[6]

Among the New Age threats to the American younger generation examined by Neil Anderson in *The Seduction of Our Children* (Harvest House 1991) is the impact of New Age ideology on education. However, in Anderson's view, that is not the only way New Age influences the class-room; 'Like many other institutions, including the US Army, public education has tapped into the human potential movement of the 1960s for cost-effective training methods that reportedly enhance class-room performance. As a result, many of our public schools are implementing techniques that are rooted in Eastern mysticism, the New Age and the occult, including guided imagery, meditation, bio-feedback, neurolinguistic programming, and various other techniques designed to reduce stress and increase concentration.' (Pages 62, 63.) In the US the case for separate Christian education is strong, and getting stronger.

Dave Hunt has said, 'It seems outrageous that in schools across America where Christian prayer has been outlawed, Yoga, Eastern meditation and visualization techniques, which are simply forms of Hindu prayer, are not only allowed, they're being actively promoted.'

The declared goal of meditation is to attain 'cosmic consciousness', oneness with all beings. 'Globalism taught in the class-room', writes Dr. Martin, 'is dangerous because it is based on a monistic world view that espouses not only the unity of all mankind but a unity of all religious beliefs too. . . . Yoga in the class-room is dangerous because all forms of yoga involve occult assumptions, even *hatha yoga*, which is often presented as a strictly physical discipline.'[7]

New Age and publishing

British Christians have been noting with concern for some time the gradual increase in the space allocated in bookshops to the 'New Age/Occult' category and the diminution of the space for Bible and Christian books. Five years ago in the USA there were 2,500 bookshops selling New Age/Occult books and no others. The number is believed to have increased considerably since then. Practically every major publisher in the USA has gone into New Age literature, though book editors, interviewed in trade journals, admit that much of it is merely 'superstition that sells'.

The upwardly mobile and sober-suited middle-aged businessmen in all Western nations are now going off on in-service courses in which the instructors use overtly spiritual techniques to enable them to handle pressure, create wealth and improve inter-personal relationships and communication.

New Age and the economy

The use of Yoga and New Age meditation techniques to 'maximize potential', improve sales techniques and enable responsible managers to cope with stress, was pioneered in the USA by a number of large corporations.

After giving a lecture to a large group in Lewisham in which I mentioned New Age meditation techniques as part of management training, a sizeable proportion of the audience gathered round to ask if I would be prepared to talk to them afterwards. Another hall was made available and we withdrew to it. The discussion lasted for some three hours. The central concern of the young men and women so eager for guidance was that, as I had been speaking, they had become aware that they were involved in the same meditation techniques I had been describing. They were Christians and concerned at the dangers of a method aimed to render their minds vacuous, 'vacant possession'. When the discussion ended each one declared his or her intention of pulling out of that particular course of management training even if it meant forgoing promotion prospects or switching companies.

Fortune magazine indicates that half of America's 500 top businesses are engaged in New Age 'human potential training' (accepted by Christians as the entering wedge to the occult). Among the companies exposing their managements to 'New Age gurus' were Pacific Bell (who had spent $173 million on 'human potential training' for their managers that involved obvious aspects of the occult), NASA, both the Ford and the General Motors car manufacturing companies, ICA, IBM, Boeing, Singer, RCA and the Bank of America. Potentially, Walter Martin believed, this gave occult forces a stranglehold on the American economy. Martin and Caryl Matriciana were also concerned that because the same techniques were being used by doctors and dentists and in the Department of the Interior, the Department of the Environment, American Customs, Army, Navy, Air Force and the Green Berets, New Age could affect almost anyone and could alter the American political agenda.[8]

Attractive faces

The point has already been made that there are many *phases* of New Age and that those involved in the primary phase may be unaware of the hard-core occult activities in which other New Agers are engaged. Many of those in the primary phase of New Age have attractive, charismatic personalities. Among these have been Elisabeth Kubler-Ross, the founder of the hospice movement, whose dizzying schedule would have felled any ordinary over-achiever. She was a trance-channeller whose beliefs were anathema to the Christian, but at least one aspect of her work was something of which Christians could approve. Fritjof

Capra, a prominent American physicist, is also one of the more attractive personalities involved in New Age. While forms of alternative medicine like *shia-tsu*, crystal healing, EST, psychic healing and acupuncture must be looked at askance by a Christian since they employ paranormal powers, other areas of alternative medicine in which New Agers are involved — including homeopathy and vegetarianism — cannot but be seen in a very positive light. If every face of New Age was repellant it would be far less dangerous.

Similarly, while stopping well short of the pantheistic New Age jargon, most Christians would sympathize with many of the objectives of the Green Party and of Greenpeace. Greenpeace, with its two and a half million supporters world-wide, affirms Mark Satin in *New Age Politics*,[9] 'is thoroughly New Age. . . . Our ultimate goal . . . is to help bring about that basic change in thinking known as "planetary consciousness".' Yet, nevertheless, second only to its health emphasis, Greenpeace must be seen as one of the most attractive and successful fronts for New Age. It is naïve to see everything in the New Age movement as thoroughly evil.

J. Z. Knight

Arguably another attractive face of New Age in the USA is honey-blond superstar channeller J. Z. Knight whose low, soft voice is like thick cream made audible. Knight, who lives in Yelm, Washington State, has made a multi-million fortune out of her New Age involvement. *Time* has termed her 'the top person's guru'. Certainly she has a direct line to the stars. Besides Shirley MacLaine, her clientele reportedly includes Bert Reynolds, Clint Eastwood, Richard Chamberlain, Shelley Fabares and Mike Farrell. Linda Evans bought a home near Knight's in order to benefit from her channelling.

Knight claims to channel Ramtha, the alleged 35,000-year-old 'ascended master' from the lost city of Atlantis. Since the beginning of the 90s thousands have packed up and moved to the rural north-west of America to survive the destruction that Ramtha has predicted will precede the 'cusp' of the millennium. Knight claims that Ramtha first appeared to her in 1977 when she was experimenting with paper pyramids in her kitchen. Like many New Agers she claims that Ramtha's spirit, not her fingers, worked the word processor when she wrote *I am Ramtha*. Thousands shell out $400 for a consultation with Knight. As a consequence she has a lavish mansion and one of the largest stables in America, Messiah Arabian Stud, Inc.

Nevertheless, interviewed on The Merv Griffin Show, Knight comes over as an attractive, personable individual with all the right attributes.

Fundamentalist Christians who attack each New Age follower *per se*, do their cause a disservice. Such attacks not infrequently enable the New Age superstar to appear the epitome of courtesy and sweet reason.

The devil always sends bitter pills sugar-coated. The tree that did the damage 'in the beginning' was not 'the tree of the knowledge of evil'. It was 'the tree of the knowledge of good and evil'.

But, with all its *phases* and *faces* — some of them attractive — there is one question we must ask of the New Age movement: *Where is it heading?* Where is it going with its many bits and pieces, uncertain borders, shifting spheres of activity and revolving cast of characters?

After the formation of the second front in World War II the armies left Normandy aiming in different directions; the British and Canadians under Montgomery, the Americans under Generals Patten, Bradley and Eisenhower. By the end of 1944 they were all in very different places. But the real question was, Where were they heading?

New Age is like that.

The people in it are all at different places. And they're not all bad places.

But the general direction is the same. And it is very dangerous indeed.

---

[1]Marilyn Ferguson, *The Aquarian Conspiracy: Personal and Social Transformation in the 1980s* (Tarcher 1980), page 364; Russell Chandler, *Understanding the New Age* (Word UK 1989) page 21; Walter Martin, *The New Age Cult* (Bethany House Publishers 1989), page 85. [2]Ibid, pages 20, 21; *Gods of the New Age*, video (Riverside Films 1984), Part 2. [3]H. J. Berry, *New Age Movement* (BTB 1988), page 39. [4]Douglas Groothuis, *Unmasking the New Age* (IVP) 1986), pages 153, 154. [5]Kenneth Wade, *Savage Future: The Sinister Side of New Age* (Autumn House 1991). [6]Walter Martin, op cit, page 58. [7]Ibid, page 61; *Gods of the New Age*, op cit. [8]David Marshall, *The Devil Hides Out* (Autumn House 1991), page 99, Walter Martin, op cit, pages 64, 71, 72; *Gods of the New Age*, op cit. [9]Delta Books, 1979, page 331.

The Arresting Case of David Icke

The experience of David Icke is a good pointer to the *direction* of New Age.

When I first became aware of him he was Coventry City goalkeeper. After it was discovered that he had rheumatoid arthritis Icke became a BBC football reporter. From the BBC he moved to become chief spokesperson of Britain's Green Party. Then he disappeared for a while.

'Son of God'

His reappearance in March 1990 was on the BBC's prime time Wogan talk show. Smiling and in a turquoise shell-suit, Icke told Wogan that he, Icke, was the son of God.[1] In the Letters page of the next week's *Radio Times* it was made clear that this had not come up in rehearsals.

'But wasn't Jesus the Son of God?' Terry hazarded. 'Oh, yes,' replied the affable Icke. 'Jesus was *a* Son of God, *a* Christ. But there have been many sons of God, many christs, and I am one.'

It was at this point that Wogan began to wilt. Either floundering or in an effort to keep the programme light, he failed to ask the right questions.

When Icke appeared on BBC's Daytime Live a few days later, Anglican interviewer Alan Titchmarsh did not make the same mistakes. The exchange went something like this:

'What makes you think you are the son of God?'

'It was revealed to me.'

'Who revealed it to you?' persisted Titchmarsh. A fleeting look of irritation passed over Icke's pleasant features.

'The masters revealed it to me.'

'What masters?'

'*The* masters, *the* christs, the enlightened ones of bygone ages.'

'You've been talking to dead people?' Titchmarsh was going to get to the bottom of this one.

'I am a channel for the spirits of the masters,' said Icke. He hadn't planned to go this far.

'A channeller. Is that the same as a medium?' asked Titchmarsh. 'How do you know that dead masters speak through you? Can you believe whatever does speak through you? Was not Jesus the unique divine Son of God? Don't spirits deceive?'

'I am a New Age channeller,' replied Icke. 'A New Age priest.' He hadn't answered the questions but he had said rather more than the New Age movement likes its up-front people to say.

Three years on, Icke was finding his 'Son of God' claim an embarrassment and beginning to retreat from it. 'New Age channeller' he is happy with.

A 'spirit-written' book

That David Icke was on our screens at all was, doubtless, to publicize his book *The Truth Vibrations* (Aquarian Press, 1990). A book which, according to its Introduction, contains 'truths' given to Icke 'by some of the most evolved beings in this solar system'. 'All the information in these pages has come through psychic communications.'

'The transformation of humankind is upon us,' wrote Icke. Evolution had moved into a new stage. There would be those who would 'tune in' to the New Age, and those who 'in the face of the spiritual truths' would cling to the old beliefs. The first new 'spiritual truth' to emerge? 'There is no such thing as death, and no matter what happens to us during our short visit to earth, we simply go back from whence we came. After a while our souls return to another physical body, usually in different circumstances, to learn more lessons and gain more experience in order to speed our evolution.' (Page 10.)

Beginning of the journey

Icke's journey to New Age priesthood had begun when his immersion in 'Green politics . . . became a spiritual journey' (page 13). He became aware that his life was being 'guided by spirits' and met others with the same awareness.

In a hotel room he asked aloud for spirits to make contact with him. First the spirits guided him to medium-cum-healer Betty Shine's book *Mind to Mind* on a railway book stand. Within twenty-four hours he had read the book, absorbed the basic beliefs of the spiritist and had set up a meeting with 45-year-old Shine.

Icke's earlier meetings with Shine were aimed at finding relief from the pain of his rheumatoid arthritis (he does not say if this relief ever came). At one meeting the 'atmosphere became charged' and the medium began to channel a Chinese mandarin, Wang Yee Lee, whose 'last life on earth was around AD 1200'. Wang's message was for Icke. The substance of it was that, in the future, there would be earthquakes in places that had not previously experienced them. As a card-carrying Green, Icke was impressed.

When, four days later, TV reported an earthquake on the Welsh border that measured 4.9 on the Richter scale, Icke felt he had all the proof he needed. He immersed himself in the writings of the sixteenth-century French psychic Michel Nostradamus (1503-66) who, it is claimed, predicted the Great Fire of London of 1666 and the rise of Adolf Hitler. In particular he homed in on those Nostradamus prophecies allegedly relating to the period 1992-2001.[2] Nostradamus, a trance-channeller in the New Age mode, had, Icke believed, predicted massive geological disruption immediately prior to the turn of the millennium. At the urging of the spirits he shared these prophecies with the Green Party Conference and with his Breakfast TV audience.

Spirit communicators

The first sign that Icke himself was developing psychic powers was when he began seeing eyes everywhere (no faces or bodies; just eyes).

Icke's spirit communicators began to set him right about God and life after death. Reincarnation and 'the law of karma' were explained to him, while God was explained away. All this, he was told, was biblical. He learned about his own past lives. He had served under Napoleon in the Moscow campaign; the scorched earth policy of the retreating Russians accounted for his 'green' views. He had been a spy in the service of Elizabeth I, and a close friend of Francis Bacon. And he believed it all!

Evil, Icke discovered, was no more than disharmony. Heaven was a state of mind. When the physical body died it went to 'the astral plain'; here the spirit had a reunion with the spirits of dead friends and relatives before being assigned to another physical body. (Presumably the dead friends and relatives the spirit met were exceptions to the reincarnation norm. . . .)

Ley-lines and chakras

Soon David Icke was hop-scotching the UK from one medium to another. He — they — were concerned with ley-lines and chakras ('energy lines on the earth's emotional body'), energy blockages and stones with psychic qualities buried in various locations. A 'pendulum' told Icke and his channeller companions which direction to take and when to stop. The stones, when found, acted 'as a sort of spiritual computer disc' (page 64). Unseen forces broke the stones into as many fragments as were necessary for the night-time, occult ceremonies in isolated hill locations. At these ceremonies 'beings from other planets . . . extraterrestrials' (page 65) were among those present.

Icke and his companions communicated frequently with their 'spirit guides' and were, from time to time, pushed or physically restrained by unseen forces. The stones which each of them carried facilitated communication with the spirit world. 'Crystals were even more useful; they do everything but talk to you . . . our relationship with the mineral kingdom will be very different in the next century' (page 67).

After a time Icke was in what he describes as 'the privileged position' of receiving information from many different spirit sources (page 73). A great global plan was revealed to him. 'Some of the communications came from the being who has the awesome responsibility of easing in and guiding the new Age of Aquarius. This is the ascended master, Rakorczy (pronounced Rakors-ski), the Lord of Civilization.' (Page 73.)

'The hierarchy'

From this spirit 'Lord', David Icke discovered that the universe was 'governed and guided' by a massive hierarchy, the personnel involved in which were selected on the basis of 'a soul's stage of evolution'. At the apex of this hierarchy was a 'Godhead' but, here as elsewhere, it is clear that this 'Godhead' is not the one revealed in the Bible. Prominent among the 'masters' who made up the 'hierarchy' were Joseph (of Joseph and Mary), Merlin (King Arthur's 'magician'), Christopher Columbus and Francis Bacon (page 74). Bacon, says Icke, was the son of Elizabeth I and Robert Dudley, Earl of Leicester, born four months after a secret wedding. . . . Determined to protect her 'virgin queen' status Elizabeth had, alleges Icke, prevented his succession. Rather predictably Icke further alleges that Bacon, not Shakespeare, 'wrote the famous plays'. . . .

Through channelling Rakorczy, Icke learned that a 'Black Sabbath' was coming to the planet. There would be terrible disease, disharmony and bloodshed. Even the earth itself had been trying to communicate this through 'crop circles'. . . . 'The Bible had been written by alchemists, magicians, seers, healers and doctors'; but it had been 'changed and misinterpreted', its secrets lost (page 83).

Channelling, tarot and crystals

By now Icke's life was densely populated by spirits. Some were visible. Others channelled through him, revealed their messages through tarot cards or crystals, or through another channeller. As a result of a message from an English-born Canadian medium (who channelled her dead mother) Icke ended up hop-scotching the ley-lines of North America, as he had done the British Isles. It was here that he learned that a new energy system would be 'imposed from the heavens' at the turn of the century, and that, to make this possible, the stars and constellations of the heavens would be moved to new positions between 1992 and 98. . . .

In a matter-of-fact sort of way Icke informs his readers; 'There are many souls who have lived on earth over thousands of years who originate from other planets. I am one of them; and so are Linda and my children. We came from a planet called Oerael in another solar system, and arrived at the start of Atlantis. Most of those working to bring in the New Age of Aquarius also came from other planets a long time ago. . . .' Migration from other planets is, apparently, possible through UFOs. . . .

It is a matter of a moment for Icke to skip from UFOs to the birth of Christ! Mary and Joseph were 'two evolved souls', 'Joseph, of course, was an aspect of Rakorczy. . . .' Jesus was not, says Icke, the result of a 'virgin birth' but was the son of Joseph born in the constellation of Virgo . . . (page 115). Icke presents Jesus as having a faulty human nature; temper, for example, 'got the better of him' when he was dealing with the money lenders. Jesus went to His death quietly because the alternative, says Icke, would have been a massive occult battle fought on the surface of the planet. The resurrection, apparently, was a myth.

ETs and the Aquarian Age

Now, as the end of the century approaches, extra-terrestrials 'are arriving on earth in large numbers' to help

New Agers defeat their enemies and facilitate 'the giant leap in evolution into the Aquarian age . . . '. Jesus Christ had heralded the Age of Pisces. This age — the age of Christian influence — would have to end decisively to make way for the inauguration of the Age of Aquarius. Hence, among the enemies of New Age needing to be defeated, were Christians who would not accept the new enlightenment! It would become more and more apparent that the most fundamental division in the world would be between 'those who are tuning in and those who are not. . . . Those racing forward spiritually and those still holding on to yesterday. It is the former group that will bring about the "cultural revolution" that Wang predicted for Britain by 1995. It will be the same in every country at some time in the next ten years. . . .'

Meanwhile, says Icke, under the New Age hierarchy of the New Age 'Godhead', the Aquarian cause would be pushed forward with every means available under the guise of 'Light to the Earth'.

In insisting on an alternative 'Godhead' Icke is not typical of New Age. Most New Agers follow Shirley MacLaine — who, in turn, follows the Buddhists — in insisting on 'the god within'. However, perhaps it is the relatively artless Icke who, by this departure, gives us the clearest indication of both the *direction* of New Age and the real power behind it. No matter how gently he puts it, it is clear from Icke's text that the destruction of Christianity is an essential prerequisite for the triumph of New Age. The apostle Paul, writing in the first century AD, believed that in the final age Satan, posing as an 'angel of light', would attempt the destruction of the cause of Christ.[3] 2 Corinthians 11: 13-15

The last time I heard David Icke featured in the media was on the Gloria Hunniford programme on Radio 4. The spirits had, apparently, instructed Icke to introduce into his home a blonde young lady. He had done so. In no time the spirits were instructing him to sleep with this young lady in the interests of 'the future of planet earth'. He had done so. And his wife, Linda, was not well pleased. Icke himself, apparently, had suffered a certain sense of guilt. This had been the cue for the spirits to communicate with him again. He should not, they told him, suffer guilt. The future of planet earth had been at stake. Quite how the planet's future had been at stake was not made clear by either the spirits or the impressionable Icke. Gloria Hunniford was amused.

Even at its occult core there is a lot of old baloney about New Age. . . .

---

[1]*The Sunday Times*, 30 August 1992, News Review, page 5. Within a year of Icke's remarkable declaration on the Wogan programme many of the pioneer leaders of Britain's Green Party had resigned believing that Icke and other high profile New Agers had robbed the party of all credibility. Sara Parkin, after twenty years with the Green (before 1985, Ecology) Party, was particularly outspoken. [2]A book emerged out of this study. V. J. Hewitt and Peter Lorie, *Nostradamus: The End of the Millennium Prophecies 1992-2001* (BCA 1992). [3]2 Corinthians 11:13-15.

New Age Fellow Travellers

'FERGIE GOES TO MYSTIC FOR HELP' trumpeted the tabloids on 13 February 1992.

Sarah, Duchess of York had, it appeared, been having secret sessions with a Greek-born 'clairvoyant and channeller' who used the names Vasso and Mrs. Kortese. Photographs were published of the Duchess emerging from Vasso's basement flat in North London and then, in public view, embracing her.

Under pressure from Fleet Street's newshounds Vasso said that she had been treating the Duchess for some time with the full approval of her husband, Prince Andrew. Rather unprofessionally, the clairvoyant-cum-healer went on; 'Her problems are pain in the back and shoulders and tensions in her private life . . . . I've met Prince Andrew.' Vasso's advertised specialities were 'hypnosis, healing and pyramid readings'.[1] A few weeks after the publicized visit to Vasso, the tabloids carried the news of the marriage break-up of the Duke and Duchess of York.

Election night

The news of the marriage collapse broke in the middle of Britain's General Election Campaign. On the evening of election day, 9 April, when millions had their radios and TVs turned on to hear the results of what promised to be the closest election in a generation, the BBC chose to put out an interview with Benjamin Creme. Creme, the wealthiest and arguably the most influential British New Ager, had paid millions of pounds to place a full-page advertisement in every Sunday newspaper exactly ten years earlier. THE CHRIST IS NOW HERE had been the burden of the advertisement. The world had seen enough of injustice and war. The Christ would go public simultaneously on every radio and TV station on 18 June (1982).

No one had held their breath. Fortunate. Nothing happened.

But, ten years on, Creme was unrepentant; the New Age, New World Order, was about to dawn. The Lord Maitreya, the New World Messiah, was waiting in the wings to reveal himself. He was the personification of the Messiah of the Jews, the returning Christ of the Christians, the Imam Mahdi of the Muslims, and the Krishna of the Hindus. He would correct every economic, social and political imbalance and injustice, end hunger and establish brotherhood. There would be one World Order with Maitreya at its head. On his emergence there would be hundreds of thousands of spontaneous healings.

The newspapers, in the ensuing days, full of the Prime Minister's triumph and the Opposition Leader's resignation, had nothing to say about Creme's messiah. But New Age beliefs continued to inform TV drama and the term 'New Age' achieved an exposure on news bulletins it had never previously enjoyed. Made and first screened in the US, New Age series 'Highway to Heaven' was being broadcast by ITV each Sunday. On 2 June, after six weeks' hype, ITV put out the home-grown 'comedy drama' *Angels*. Basic to it was the no-death view of New Age; the 'dead' both observed and visited the living, even interfering with their lives. The 'dead' mixed freely with the living, feeding information to them from the 'other side'. *Angels* had a larger viewing audience than any other TV drama put out in Britain during the summer of 92. 'New Age has taken the entertainment scene and the media by storm.'[2]

New Age travellers

But not all New Agers were well pleased by the appropriation of the term 'New Age' to between ten and twenty thousand travellers who, in the course of the summer, moved around southern England and the Welsh border lands. With their ramshackle buses and assorted other conveyances, they appeared on TV news bulletins clogging the roads between Malvern and Ludlow, Derbyshire and Devon, Stonehenge and Glastonbury, moved on by police and harried by locals. To the naked eye they looked like a vast hippy commune transplanted from the sixties and, when they struck camp, their 'festivals' appeared indistinguishable from the sixties' pop concerts. As in the earlier decade, dealers were on the fringes supplying drugs to those who wanted and could pay for them. Admission prices for the festivals had increased; £49 a head was the asking price for admission to the Glastonbury Festival at the summer solstice.[3]

Those concerned to give New Age an intellectual image and a cut-glass accent, sought to distance themselves from the revellers on the move. Nevertheless there was much to tie them in with the mass movement. As I moved among the ten-thousand-strong 'convoy' temporarily (and illegally) camped at Piltdown, Somerset, their talk was of astrology, and the writings of New Age superstars. However, they seemed to have thrown up their own gurus rather than imported them. Primal religion was the order of the day. Druids rather than Buddhas.

For Jem, 31, Madonna counted for more than any New Age messiah. In his scheme of things she stood for everything that was the antithesis of Christianity. Jesus was the sacred, Madonna the profane; and Jem was all for the profane. He had not heard of the Lord Maitreya. The inside of Jem's (circa 1959) caravan was plastered with Madonna and Elvis Presley posters. Presley, he maintained, was still alive.

Jesus had a hostile press in another caravan where Jed, 20, lived with Samantha, 31, and her three well-dressed children. On the table, to my surprise, was a copy of Barbara Thiering's anti-Christian polemic *Jesus the Man*. Having part-read the book Jed pronounced that there had been no resurrection and that Jesus had died a natural death in AD64. Samantha, who had been to America, had jaundiced views of Christianity — having witnessed phoney healings and the preaching of evangelist Morris Cerullo — and her life-view combined anarchism with a belief in 'the god within'. Ed, 19, looked for a new world leader, 'a world guru'; 'yes, a dictator, if necessary'.

The impression left by my Piltdown interviews, as by my interviews with more usual New Agers on two university campuses, is that the typical New Ager is a butterfly. He/she flits from healing therapies like Reiki, aromatherapy or acupuncture to the 'newest' idea in the latest spirit-written book to the Gnostic gospels; then on to reincarnation and an absorption in digging up past lives through recall therapies. But the end of the metamorphosis is always the same: channelling the spirits or some other form of hardcore occult activity.

Genta, who claimed to have taken a Third in Sociology from Reading, was heavily into New Age. She gave the impression that, for her, even excitement had become boring. It was clear that she was held in awe by other travellers at Piltdown and, within the convoy, moved from group to group feeding at the expense of others. One of her detractors told me, 'Her need for control makes Stalin look a wimp.' Coming close in appearance to the sixties' hippy stereotype, Genta told me; 'Global transformation is what it's all about. All is one and all is god. Man must pursue enlightenment through communion with the higher self, the divine spark within him. This will lead to self-transformation and, in the end, the transformation of the planet. Christianity is worn out, threadbare. Aquarian concepts, first developed in the seventies, matured and expanded by the spirit-written books of the eighties, will be the basis of the world-view of the next millennium.'

There was more of the same.

Like Alice Bailey and Benjamin Creme, Genta was a channeller of Djwhal Khul.

Genta must take the credit for providing me with the incentive — based on New Age books and interviews with coherent New Agers — to isolate the beliefs that are quintessentially New Age. Then, setting aside what has, only in recent times, made some of them into the fads and fetishes of the famous, run them down to source.

So what *are* the key concepts of New Age? And what history, if any, did they have before the sixties and seventies?

To distil New Age down to a sort of creed of essentials proved harder than I expected. But, once done, to separate new concepts from old was not so difficult. Most interesting was how many New Age ideas *are* old. Even more interesting was *how* old the core-concepts proved to be.

---

[1]*Daily Record*, 13 February 1992. [2]John Drane, *What is the New Age saying to the Church?* (Marshall Pickering 1991), page 14. [3]See *The Observer*, 31 May 1992; *The Sunday Express*, 9 August 1992.

Designer Religion

C. S. Lewis said that at the last ditch the final conflict between religions would have Hinduism and Christianity as the only viable alternatives. Hinduism, because it absorbed all other religious systems. Christianity, because it excluded all others, maintaining the supremacy of the claims of Jesus Christ.

Bits and pieces

In the West for Hinduism we can read New Age. New Age is the ultimate *syncretism;*[1] absorbing and attempting to reconcile so wide a spectrum of beliefs, religions, practices, theories and superstitions that it has almost as many faces as adherents. In an address to Senior Evangelical Anglican clergy at Swanwick Dr. Robert Runcie said; 'Saying anything too precise about the New Age movement is liable to give it a coherence which it does not possess . . . . (It) is *eclectic*[2] because it takes bits and pieces from various philosophies and religions in an uncritical way . . . . (It) takes eclecticism a stage further since it demands that different religions place their beliefs alongside one another in a complementary way' with a view to 'harmonizing' them.[3]

As Lewis pointed out, it is impossible to 'harmonize' Christianity with other religions in this way. For this reason New Age borrows ideas from virtually every system *except* Christianity. Though, having said that, it *is* possible to find early-phase New Agers sucking certain pseudo-Christian ideas in — especially from the Gnostic 'gospels' — and adding them to their heady mixture of pop spirituality. But the Christian ideas are from Gnosticism or have been misconstrued, most often wrenched from their context.

New Age: Where does it come from?

It is easier to list the main sources from which New Agers have borrowed their beliefs than to list the beliefs themselves.

In the early sixties choices seemed to be simpler than now; my own choice seemed to be between Christianity on the one hand, and various forms of materialism on the other. Ever since the sixties we have lived in a sort of supermarket of world views. Hence choices have become more complex. Just as you can chose from a range of different washing powders, so you can chose from a range of different understandings of the world. And, as with washing powders, each 'understanding' has its own advertisers assuring us that this particular brand is 'the best'. Assailed by such an assortment the ordinary person is bewildered.

Churchmen have contributed to this bewilderment. They have attacked the Bible and laid aside its Gospel. A school of liberal churchmen have sought themselves to popularize syncretistic views. John Hick, for example, tells us that Christ is only one way to God, and that Christians should abandon their adversarial stance against other great world faiths like Buddhism, Islam and Hinduism, and regard them instead as allies in a common mission. He tells us that in Chicago is a Baha'i temple. Its nine entrances each bear the name of a different spiritual 'master', including Christ. The nine aisles all lead to the same central altar. Hick uses this as an illustration of his point that 'all roads lead to God'.

Until the relatively-recent past 'trendy', 'liberal' clergymen of many mainstream denominations were advancing opinions like this. Then suddenly they stopped. Too late they realized that their all-roads-lead-to-God theology had cleared the space for New Age to enter the picture.

New Age is 'designer religion', satanically tailored for our age. It borrows ideas from a whole range of world views on sale in the supermarket:

ASTROLOGY. It has taken on board the whole kit-and-caboodle of astrology. Even its name is borrowed from astrology.

ECOLOGY. To quote Runcie; 'New Age finds a focus in a vague discontent with the existing order of the universe and within the human spirit. It tends to find its main expression politically in the green movement . . . . Yet many members and supporters of the Green Party would not be New Agers . . . . '[4] From the green movement New Age borrows a reverence for the natural environment — but takes it to a point where it becomes, for many New Agers, pantheism. 'Creation' and 'nature' are abiding concerns of all New Agers. There is a tendency to *personalize* nature; expressions like 'Mother Earth', 'The Good Earth' recur in New Age literature and, while New Ager David Icke believes in an alternative 'godhead' and New Ager Shirley MacLaine (typical of many others) believes in 'the god within', many New Age speeches, books and pamphlets convey the idea that god-is-in-everything (pantheism).

HOMEOPATHY. From homeopathic medicine New Age borrows a number of quite sound ideas — but weaves them about in such a way that they become part of an obsession with the human body that borders on body worship. New age is *holistic* in a number of senses. It wants to see the removal of all the boundaries in the world, religious and national, and it wants to bring mind, body and spirit together in a 'whole person' concept of the individual. There is a tremendous commitment to fringe medicine and various forms of therapy and pseudo-psychology. There is a longing to be in touch with powerful forces in the universe excluded or condemned by the Judaeo-Christian tradition. These forces include the energy 'ley lines', a concept borrowed from primal religion, and the spirit world.

HINDUISM. From Hinduism it borrows reincarnation and meditation techniques: reincarnation disposes of sin and judgement by offering a whole series of lifetimes in which to work off a negative 'karma'; and meditation techniques are used to make the mind 'vacant possession'.

Maharishi Mahesh Yogi's transcendental meditation and Werner Erhard's 'EST' are important strains in New Age.

BUDDHISM. From Buddhism New Age borrows the abandonment of God in favour of the 'god deep down in every individual', and calls the pursuit of this 'god' 'enlightenment'.

EVOLUTION. The concept of evolution is basic to all New Age literature. New Age adapts the Darwinian concept to accommodate the idea that an elite can evolve to a higher state in which, as 'enlightened ones', they enjoy certain advantages over others, principally psychic abilities.

SPIRITISM. From spiritism New Age borrows so much that some writers have seen it as merely the latest manifestation of the old cult. Certainly many of the ideas borrowed from the Eastern religions are used to rationalize involvement in the spirit world, the occult. But, as in other cases, New Age terminology is a little different from the vocabulary of its precursor. New Agers advance the view that living 'enlightened ones' become 'channellers' (not mediums) for dead 'enlightened ones', 'masters'. Channellers are 'a step up the occult ladder from mediums, channellers claim their bodies are taken over by the "entities" or spirits from another dimension'.[5]

SATANISM AND WITCHCRAFT. Insofar as New Age advances the idea that an individual can and should be 'possessed' by a spirit or spirits, and that he can and should live his life to serve the spirit or spirits, it must be said that New Age has a debt to satanism. Further, insofar as New Age, beginning with the premise 'You are god' advances the idea that all restraints upon behaviour can be abandoned as and when it suits the individual or group, it must be said that it shares something with witchcraft.

New Age is 'new' in its vocabulary and style; but its ideas and practices are as old as the Eastern religions of Hinduism and Buddhism, Western occultism and the mystical oracles of ancient Greece and Egypt. 'New Age has simply recast the theory of reincarnation into the language of Western humanistic psychology, science and technology.'[6] It has been argued that because of the astrological connection the cult also holds historical ties with Sumerian, Chaldean, Babylonian and Persian religious practices.[7]

Basic beliefs

Now, having emphasized the diversity of New Age, stressed the multiplicity of sources from which its beliefs are drawn, and conceded that it has many *faces* (fronts) and *phases* (degrees of involvement), let us attempt a list of New Age beliefs. This list is drawn from scores of interviews with 'New Agers' (some of them conducted before the term 'New Age' gained currency in the mid seventies; most of them belonging to the late eighties and early nineties) and my reading of New Age texts by authors such as Marilyn Ferguson, Ruth Montgomery, Benjamin Creme, Shirley MacLaine, Jane Roberts, David Spangler and David Icke.[8]

1. ABOUT GOD. Most New Age authors accept the Buddhist view of 'the god within'. Literature by 'green' New Agers assumes the 'god-is-in-everything' (pantheistic) view. A minority believe in a 'godhead' as the apex of the New Age hierarchy made up of masters (enlightened ones). Benjamin Creme has written; 'In a sense there is no such thing as God. God does not exist. And in another sense there is nothing else but God, only God exists . . . . All is God. And because all is God, there is no God.'[9]

[handwritten margin note: Christianity there is only one God]

2. ABOUT CHRIST. New Agers use the term 'christ' interchangeably with 'master'. This, of course, implies that there have been many christs/masters: the enlightened ones of past ages who are now dead. New agers take the view that Jesus — to them one of many christs — had a 'fallen, sinful nature' but, nevertheless, ultimately attained to perfection. David Spangler has written; 'Jesus won his christship by a strenuous life.' He also speaks of Christ as an example, 'the christ pattern'.

3. ABOUT THE ATONEMENT. Most Christians believe that Jesus — the perfect, unique Son of God — died on the cross for man's sin. Theologians call this 'the substi-

tutionary death'. New Agers make much mileage out of attacking the substitutionary death of Christ, the blood atonement, as 'a primitive notion'. God would not, they argue, place the sins of the world on the shoulders of His sinless Son. Insofar as the concept of 'salvation' enters into New Age literature, it is a state to be deserved through perfect, enlightened living. <u>The concept of unmerited pardon (grace) is foreign to New Agers</u>.

4. ABOUT MAN. New Agers argue that man is basically good but his present karma stands in the way of true self-realization, goodness. Man is responsible for the circumstances in which he lives in the present, and in which he will live in the future.

5. ABOUT DEATH. There is no death; just a perpetual cycle of reincarnation governed by the law of karma.

6. ABOUT SIN AND JUDGEMENT. To the New Ager, these notions are dispensed with through reincarnation. Any 'negative karma' that an individual acquires in one lifetime can be worked off in a future reincarnation. Since god is 'within', the individual can, to a significant degree, determine what is right or wrong for himself.

7. ABOUT THE WORLD. The New Agers' world view is monistic (all is one) or pantheistic (all is God). The oneness of all things is called Ultimate Reality. The world and evil are not part of the Reality and hence are an illusion. Only spirit and good are Reality. 'The idea that "all is one" is foundational for the New Age,' writes Douglas Groothuis in *Unmasking the New Age* (IVP 1986), pages 18, 19. 'It permeates the movement in all its various manifestations — from holistic health to the new physics, from politics to transpersonal psychology, from Eastern religions to the occult. . . . Good and evil are really one and the same.' The influence of monism on contemporary American thinking has been such that H. J. Berry has remarked, 'The world-view in the United States has switched from the atheism of secular humanism (man is the measure of all things) to the pantheism of the New Age movement (man — and everything else — is god).'

New Age Movement (BTB 1988), page 14.

8. ABOUT THE FUTURE. Psychics (those who have attained to a higher level of evolution), in co-operation with 'extraterrestrials', will usher in the New Age, the Age of Aquarius. Some say by the end of the twentieth century. Others by the year 2050. Still others by the year 2064. Global transformation will be achieved, in the ultimate, when all humans undergo self-transformation. This self-transformation will lead to oneness.

David Spangler writes, 'As we enter into the New Age, what we are entering into is a cycle, a period of time, a period of unfoldment when . . . humanity . . . is the world's saviour, and ultimately it is upon the shoulders of humanity that the future and the translation for the entry into light . . . rests.' He further argues that the Findhorn community on the Moray Firth in Scotland 'represents the second coming. Any individual, any centre, who so embodies the new that it becomes a magnetic source to draw the new out of the rest of the world, embodies the second coming.'[10]

Benjamin Creme believes that the Lord Maitreya has held the hierarchic office of 'christ' for 2,600 years (and that Jesus was his disciple). He further believes that the Lord Maitreya will — with the other christs or masters — physically reveal himself at some time in the course of the next half century.[11]

9. ABOUT DEMONS. New Agers believe that Satan or Lucifer has been given a bad press by the Bible, and that it is not his intention to lead man down the path of wrongdoing. There is no Satan and there are no demons as far as New Agers are concerned. 'Man is his own satan, just as man is his own salvation. . . . The forces of evil are part of God.'[12]

10. ABOUT TRUTH. New Agers teach that there is no such thing as absolute truth.

How new is New Age?

A *Time* magazine feature on New Age concluded: 'So

here we are in the New Age, a combination of spirituality and superstition, fad and farce, about which the only thing certain is that it is not new.'[13]

The debt of the New Age movement to astrology, Hinduism and Buddhism, as we have seen, makes its key concepts thousands of years old.

We have the nineteenth century's Helena Petrovna Blavatsky and the Theosophical Society to thank for the Westernization of Hindu philosophy and its marriage with spiritism and the occult. Blavatsky was the link between nineteenth-century Spiritism and the twentieth-century New Age in that she argued that the dead people whose spirits she channelled were also the source of cosmic wisdom. She claimed that her 1,200-page *Isis Unveiled* had been 'dictated by the Masters of Wisdom via astral light and spirit guides'.

The occult itself reaches back into Old Testament times. We read of King Saul consulting a witch and participating in a seance. We also read many long and detailed condemnations of occult practices. However, hands-on contact with the spirit world in the modern West would appear to have begun on 20 December 1835 by Emily Pearcefield, a member of The Shakers. More familiar is the occasion when, in a modest clapboard homestead in Hydesville, New York State, on 31 March 1848, John and Margaret Fox and their daughters Margaret and Kate worked out their morse code with the spirit world.[14] The spirit world's response was such that modern spiritism was launched. Seances for communicating with 'the spirits of the dead' became an obsession, first in the USA, then in Europe.

Alice Bailey, who died in 1949, is believed by New Agers to have been the first 'modern channeller'. She claimed to channel a spirit called Djwhal Khul. Since Bailey's death Benjamin Creme has assumed her mantle.

In one of the most succinct summaries of contemporary New Age belief and practice Brooks Alexander states, 'The entities (spirits) endlessly repeat the primal lie, the threefold creed of error: There is no death; man is God; knowledge of self is salvation.'[15] At least two of the three elements in this primal lie — '*You will not surely die. . . . You will be like God*'[16] — came from the devil and date from the dawn of time.

---

[1]Syncretism: Noun. Attempted reconciliation of conflicting beliefs. [2]Eclectic: Adjective. Taking from a variety of sources that which is best suited to one's own purposes. [3]Robert Runcie, 'A Response to the New Age', *Christian Weekly*, 24 November 1989. *Christian Weekly* has now been absorbed by *The Church of England Newspaper*. [4]Ibid. [5]George Hackett, 'Ramtha, a Voice from Beyond', *Newsweek*, 15 December 1986, page 42. [6]Russell Chandler, *Understanding the New Age* (Word 1989), page 18. [7]Walter Martin, *The New Age Cult* (Bethany House 1989), page 15. [8]Marilyn Ferguson, *The Aquarian Conspiracy* (1980); Ruth Montgomery, *Aliens Among Us* (1985); Benjamin Creme, *The Reappearance of The Christ and The Masters of Wisdom* (1989); Shirley MacLaine, *Out on a Limb, Dancing in the Light, Going Within;* Jane Roberts, *The Seth Material* (1987); David Spangler, *Explorations* (1980); David Icke, *The Truth Vibrations* (1990). [9]Benjamin Creme, op cit, page 110. [10]David Spangler, op cit, pages 6, 10, 11, 13. [11]Creme, op cit, page 30. [12]Spangler, op cit, page 39. [13]*Time*, 7 December 1987, page 62. [14]Jerome Clark, *1844: Religious Movements, Mental Phenomena and Psychic Cults* (SPA 1968), pages 346 *et seq*. [15]Brooks Alexander, 'Theology from the Twilight Zone', *Christianity Today*, 18 September 1987, page 25. [16]Genesis 3:4, 5, NIV.

The Lure of the Psychic

So one thing you cannot say about New Age is that it is new.

A black American basketball coach said, 'New Age is a vacuum cleaner. It picks up whatever is there and messes it all up. So, when you open the bag, you recognize all the bits and pieces there are in there — but the mixture is completely different from anything you've ever seen before. You probably wonder how it can all possibly belong together. The fact is, it doesn't.'[1]

Clientele of 'Beautiful People'

That notwithstanding, it is the magnet for a large and most surprising clientele. . . .

Tom Cruise and his wife Nicole Kidman personify everything that is glamorous about Hollywood. And 'the hottest double act since Bogart and Bacall' have turned to Scientology, one of the harder nuggets in the New Age flow labelled by a British high court 'obnoxious, corrupt, sinister and dangerous'.[2]

Also drawn into New Age in its various forms are John Travolta, Dennis Weaver, Sharon Stone, Mimi Rogers, Kirstie Alley, Demi Moore and Emilio Estevez — all from the world of the silver screen. They join a long list of show business people like Placido Domingo Jun., Linda Blair, Sonny Bono, Priscilla Presley and her daughter Lisa Marie. Anyone working in close proximity to these New Age stars — especially in their homes — can expect to be sacked and replaced by one of the faithful if they do not show speedy signs of conversion. . . .[3]

Britain's Derek Jameson, one time editor of the *Daily Express* and now co-presenter with his wife Ellen of the twice-weekly BBC Radio 2 programme 'The Jamesons', regularly dispenses New Age 'wisdom' over the air waves, interspersed with music. The Monday and Thursday programmes frequently feature the paranormal. Ellen is often heard recommending the use of crystals to those who write in to the programme.

In the run-up to the US election in November 1992 the victorious contender claimed to be in the habit of 'speaking to Elvis'. President Clinton was, of course, aware that Elvis Presley had been dead for sixteen years. No one batted an eyelid at his assertion since a quasi-religious cult has developed around 'the King'. Though brought up a Christian, Presley was introduced by Larry Geller to the writings of Alice Bailey. As a result of his reading, and a vision he claimed to have received, Presley reached the view that he was a 'buddha' or 'a Maitreya' in the years before his death. Hence the cult.[4]

Chic to be 'spiritual'

It's chic to have something of the spiritual about you in the nineties. 'More spirituality and less materialism is what we need in the West,' writes actress Joanna Lumley. 'In the nineties we're going to start finding our souls again. . . .'[5] The radical materialism of the eighties was provoking a reaction even when it seemed that everyone was worshipping mammon. Whether it was Reaganism, or Thatcherism or Milton Friedmanism (or simply pre-Keynsian economics by any other name) it was not an adequate diet for the human spirit. In the East regimes were toppling from Estonia to Tirana as peoples reacted against Communism towards Christianity. In the West the reaction to radical materialism took the form of an increased involvement in the occult in its various forms.

Seasoned observers had to pinch themselves when V. J. Hewitt and Peter Lorie, claiming to have cracked his code, made the prophecies of the sixteenth-century psychic Michel Nostradamus (1503-66) a best-seller. People were apparently eager to read that these prophecies had a particular application to the last decade of the twentieth century and that in that decade an earthquake would devastate

California (1993), it would be discovered that sound waves can kill cancer (1993), a new hole would be discovered in the ozone layer (1995), aliens would be televised (1998) and a 'New World Religion' would be established (2000).[6]

In Western Australia, Prasada Hamilton has published the New Age equivalent of *Yellow Pages: The Blue Pages*. This New Age directory offers a bewildering array of options to those reacting against materialism and in search of spiritual fulfilment in the form of 'personal transformation' and 'self discovery'. Included among the services listed are those of trans-personal psychologists, Eastern gurus, Gnostic priests, and those who can heal you with crystals and advise you on making contact with entities from the spirit world.

Reaction against radical materialism

Before the late sixties there would have been few takers for these services. Numbers would have increased through the seventies. But it has taken the radical materialism of the eighties to give such services volume appeal and to make New Age, of which they are aspects, a mass movement. 'It is now time', says Stirling University's Dr. John Drane, 'for a more spiritual way of life that will see us safely through the nineties, and on into a new century and the next millennium.'[7]

So, then, what was wrong with materialism?

1. ROOTLESSNESS. Its 'consumables' were surface things and it left man rootless. Roots anchor, nourish and, to some extent, explain an individual. Intellectually, rootlessness fosters gullibility: the first essential for the reception of the unreason of New Age. Morally, rootlessness implants the notion that the deadliest of all sins is to be different: New Age rationalizes the sexual revolution. Emotionally, rootlessness is a sense of not belonging: New Age provides the feeling that an individual belongs to a continuum that links him with the psychic 'enlightened ones' of all ages.

2. AIMLESSNESS. Humanity's most obvious missing component is a built-in direction finder. Materialism means that if an individual's life should miss its planned trajectory, go off course, then it is destroyed. Further, it means that even if the trajectory is adhered to, there is a life-stage when the individual is forced to acknowledge that the sky is not the limit, that success is a relative term and of no consequence since life has no meaning.

Writing of the appeal of the occult in the 1930s, 'New Age' author Aldous Huxley describes how 'modern man moves through life hollow with pointlessness, trying to fill the void within him by external stimuli . . . '. By this he meant the fodder served up by the entertainment media to provide a daily ration of excitement for minds dulled by repetitive work, trivial interests, and vacant goals. As Huxley well knew, under these circumstances, the individual will latch on to *any* explanation of life rather than live with none. And, further, if, beyond vicarious living, he gets wind of an occult world in which he can become directly involved, he is a ready prey.

3. LOSTNESS. Almost an assumption of Western materialism in the eighties was that the landmarks and guideposts of the past had been destroyed. The sixties' and seventies' generations had, sometimes rebelliously, sometimes irresponsibly, often in the name of a specious freedom, destroyed or obscured the signposts, boundaries and moral road-warnings of Christian society. An individual who is lost for want of signposts is likely to strike out in *any* direction, rather than stand still. If, in a materialistic wilderness, a mirage should appear in one direction, an individual who is consciously or unconsciously 'lost' is likely to walk towards it.

4. LONELINESS. The replacement of communities by conurbations, the weakening of family life through increasing sexual freedom and the very self-centredness fundamental to materialism, make for loneliness and individual isolation (not necessarily the same thing). The lonely and isolated, like the rootless, yearn to belong. For them any group or

'ism' has an attraction — more especially if it is offering self-knowledge and 'enlightenment'.

5. <u>DISINTEGRATION</u>. By the eighties the old moral pattern of life had, it appeared, disintegrated. With all its faults, it had held life together within a framework of consistent and widely-held principles of conduct that had given society order and harmony. This disintegration, together with the supposed dangers of repression, had released disruptive forces: instinct, passion, selfishness, rebelliousness. These had created bewilderment and distraction.

Paul Tillich listed these symptoms of spiritual dissolution: 'The disrupted, split, disintegrated personality, the hidden will to death, the torturing anxiety, the dread despair, the mental cleavage, the compulsions, neurotic trends, unconscious strivings, restlessness . . . hostility against ourselves. . . .'

All this created a climate that would have facilitated the triumph of *any* movement built on emotion, unreason. In the event, it was New Age and the occult.

The tragedy is that New Age has no cure for rootlessness, no answer to aimlessness, no satisfying destination for lostness, can only exacerbate loneliness — and complete disintegration.

Before we turn our back on Christianity in favour of Eastern philosophy, we owe it to ourselves to examine the religion of Jesus Christ.

The occult world is dark and, in the darkness, there are many shapes. What *are* these shapes? Can we know? Can we afford to tread the darkness without knowing?

There *is* nothing new about New Age. The lies on which the occult world is based are almost as old as time. If, far older than time, there is an all-knowing, all-loving God who explained the occult world and identified the menacing shapes it contains, do we not owe it to ourselves to examine His explanation?

The world of New Age is an occult world in which

every aspect of life is governed and manipulated by the spirits. Will Baron found that out.

[1]Cited John Drane, *What Is the New Age Saying to the Church?* (Marshall Pickering 1991), pages 15, 16. [2]*Sunday Express*, 19 July 1992, page 48. [3]Ibid, pages 48, 49. [4]*Church of England Newspaper*, 30 October 1992, page 17. [5]*Stare Back and Smile* (1990), page 9. See Kenneth Wade, *Savage Future: The Sinister Side of New Age* (Autumn House 1991), pages 38-41 on Dennis Weaver. [6]V. J. Hewitt and Peter Lorie, *Nostradamus. The End of Millennium Prophecies* (BCA 1992). [7]John Drane, op cit, page 15.

Hardcore Occult and Beyond

A great deal of baloney is talked and written by New Agers. New Age is a designer religion for an age of unreason. But at its centre is hardcore occult activity. The reaction against Western materialism has taken the form of a reaction towards the occult.

New Age priest

Will Baron's *Deceived by the New Age: the Story of a New Age Priest* is, without question, the most successful book against New Age written from a Christian perspective. Not surprising, this. For nine years Baron was as involved in New Age as it is possible to be. But he lived to come out the other side, be converted to Christianity — and to tell the story.

Will Baron's case study had featured in *The Devil Hides Out*. I was aware that he had come to be accepted by American Christians as *the* authority on New Age, having appeared repeatedly on Pat Robertson's TV programme and having featured in a raft of documentaries on both radio and TV. However, I had not met him. From reading his book, many questions remained in my mind. In Britain to visit his parents, Will set aside 6 October 1992 for an in-depth interview with me. Right off let me say that Will is one of the most interesting people I have ever met. Further to that, a few hours' exposure to him gave me more fresh insights into New Age than could have been gleaned from a shelf-ful of books — whether by Christians or New Agers.

The value of Will Baron's testimony, obviously, is that *he* has the inside story. I put it to him that, having covered his case in my first book, I had been looking for another New Ager converted to Christianity to feature in my second. I had not found one. I asked Will, 'Are you one of a kind?'

Will's reply somewhat unnerved me; 'You could say so. Randall Baer's book *Inside the New Age Nightmare*

(Huntingdon House) is certainly the story of a New Age channeller who became a Christian. It is still selling well in the States. The sad thing is, though, that two days after the book's official publication Randall drove his car over a 300-ft cliff. There was no suicide note, and the police found no evidence of mechanical failure. They're still baffled. . . .'

After explaining in some detail the nature of 'channelling', the influence of Eastern religion and meditation techniques, and the function of the 'masters', I was interested to find out from Will how he had become involved in New Age in the first place.

He had, he said, been little influenced by his Christian upbringing. A health problem had made him interested in alternative healing. He had seen an advertisement for 'Health for the New Age'. He had visited a centre in Addison Crescent, Kensington, operated by Lieutenant Colonel Marcus McClauseland.

After we had established that, I was interested in what had brought about the transition from alternative medicine to hardcore occult. 'The transition, for me,' said Baron, 'came as a result of my interest in mental, as well as physical, health: whole-person health. From Kensington I went to a Primal Therapy Centre at Burtonport, Donegal. The centre was called "Atlantis". There I had my astrological chart drawn up and interpreted. That was my first involvement in the "mystical dimension".'

From his book I was aware that most of Will's story was based around Los Angeles. I wanted to know at what point this not untypical 'Lancashire lad' had found his way to the US of A. He explained; 'From "primal therapy" I graduated to "feeling therapy" and crossed to Findhorn. Findhorn has courses in all aspects of New Age from the teachings of the most fashionable (living) guru to channelling dead "masters".' From Findhorn, Baron had crossed over to a 500-strong New Age community in California. This community, like others, existed because New Agers believed that there was no point — whatever therapy they might have followed — achieving 'a sane, neurosis-free personality to live in an insane, neurosis-ridden world'. Hence the need for an all-New Age environment. 'Ironically, after twelve years' existence, the community I joined collapsed because of law suits!' said Will. 'But before it collapsed I already knew that I wanted more than psycho-therapy. I wanted to immerse myself in the mystical world. That's how come I joined the "Lighted Way" community in Los Angeles and met Muriel.'

Muriel, I recalled from Baron's book, was his 60-year-old, blonde American guru; his mentor. Under Muriel's instruction Baron had become a channeller and disciple of Djwhal Khul. His whole life had come to centre around the presence of, and communication with, spirits. He had immersed himself in esoteric literature and, under the constant direction of 'the masters', become a New Age priest.

When Djwhal Khul had first materialized before Baron it had been as 'a shining person radiating intense golden-white light.'[1] Straight-backed and cross-legged, Baron had kept in touch with his spirit 'master' through meditation. Djwhal Khul had become a mysterious, enveloping force from which it had become impossible to escape day or night. Nevertheless, in common with David Icke, Baron had come to believe that Djwhal Khul was one of the 'masters' of a New Age hierarchy at the apex of which was an alternative 'Godhead'.

After Baron had explained 'channelling' and the 'voices' that routinely spoke to him in the course of his New Age life, I was concerned with what he had actually *seen* of paranormal phenomena. 'That's an interesting one,' he said. 'Muriel always saw what looked like a flesh-and-blood man sitting or standing in the room. What *I* saw was a sort of "visionary experience". I was awake but I could see it whether my eyes were opened or closed. You could say that it was rather like looking at an image on a movie screen. When I stopped channelling Djwhal Khul and, on the instructions of Muriel, began to channel another spirit called "Jesus Christ", things were different. While the voice of "Jesus Christ" was audible, I *saw* nothing at all.'

Had he ever been *really* scared?

'Not *really*. At no stage did any terrifying images manifest themselves in my home. Even when I received a "shaking" in the night and a spirit voice began to speak to me it wasn't *really* scary. The devil is more subtle than that. If demons went around scaring people out of their wits, they would drive them into the arms of the *real* Jesus Christ. The devil doesn't want that. It is not in his interest to terrify. Remember too, good is infinitely stronger than evil and God is all-powerful.'

This response interested me. In the interviews I had conducted with New Agers, and in the published testimonies of New Agers, I had found that only a minority would admit that psychic or paranormal phenomena had actually scared them. Will was with the majority. The fact is, of course, that those terrified by the horrors from Satan's nightmare dimension rarely go into print. Studies of Spiritists indicate that a high proportion actually end their days as suicides or in psychiactric hospitals. The case studies examined in *The Devil Hides Out* had been, largely, of occultists who *were* terrified by the shapes in the darkness. For some, like Johanna Michaelson in *The Beautiful Side of Evil* (Harvest House), the worst terrors were experienced when moves were made away from occultism to the Cause of Christ. Clearly the devil uses terror when it suits him — but not against those who have made a total surrender to Christ (that God would not allow) or against those he wants to make use of (that would not be in his interests).

Findhorn revisited

Will found, however, that the spirits were not without their nuisance value, and that they could use 'frighteners' to achieve their ends.

In Los Angeles Baron had little money. What he did have he gave to support the New Age cause. But the spirits were constantly demanding more and, according to the testimony of his book, applying pressure — I should have said 'frighteners' — when he did not immediately come up with the sum demanded. When the spirits told him to move house, Baron moved house. When they told him to take a vow of celibacy and live alone, he followed their directions. In isolation, his 'third-eye centre — the chakra located in the forehead' was 'opened'. Thereafter his life was constantly haunted with paranormal phenomena; manifestations and spirit voices predicting, directing, governing.

Baron was told to move back to London. It was in a London hotel that he was 'blitzed' by a 'blast of energy' that almost destroyed him. The devil can gauge, apparently, the level of terror required to achieve the desired result. . . . Baron fell to his knees as though he had been sprayed with bullets. A deafening voice — he took it to be the voice of 'the Godhead' — directed him to return to Findhorn, Scotland. In print Baron describes Findhorn as 'the Vatican City of the New Age movement'.[2]

At Findhorn, says Baron, 'Satan has built a paradise for his New Age followers.' The substance of this 'paradise'? An extensive mobile home and trailer park with gardens and community buildings, plus an eighty-seven-room hotel that looks like a castle and contains a vast auditorium and a publishing house. In addition, the Findhorn estate includes a number of other very large houses set in their own grounds. It has 9,000 visitors a year, currently has a £500,000 extension plan, has been at the centre of a £5 million housing development controversy and is deeply resented by the local community.[3]

Will Baron confirmed that Findhorn has been able to improve its image considerably in the last ten years. When I had first visited it in 1980 to conduct interviews, the atmosphere of evil had almost been palpable. While 'on campus' I had witnessed examples of 'psychic intuition'. The place had seemed to be densely populated with hippy-types of various ages, some of whom, I had thought at the time, were either under the influence of drugs or actually mind-controlled by the spirits even as I spoke to them.[3]

Over the years it would appear that Findhorn has had the 'Saatchi and Saatchi treatment'. When, ten years after my first visit, anti-occult campaigner Kevin Logan, his £180 fee paid for by Reachout Trust, had taken a course at Findhorn, he had derived quite a different impression from mine. The clientele, then, had been drawn from a wide social spectrum and he had been treated with both respect and tolerance.[4]

When I received a long and abusive letter — every third word underlined — from a Torquay medium on 10 August 1992 accusing me of doing Findhorn an injustice in a magazine article, I decided to betake me north-wards. She had, she said, never been to Findhorn but had heard excellent reports of it from fellow mediums and channellers. Hence, to set the record straight, let it be stated that the place *does* have a different ambience these days. I suspect that what they are aiming for is an atmosphere somewhere between a redbrick university and a theological seminary. After a dozen years, however, the major difference discernable at Findhorn is the extent of its plant and the size (as well as type) of its clientele. Findhorn is going from strength to strength. Will Baron confirmed this in his interview with me.

When Will Baron returned to Findhorn he was treated as a privileged insider. He remained there for six months. And during this period he saw what Kevin Logan failed to see. 'Saatchi and Saatchi' (or equivalent) notwithstanding, Findhorn provides training in all types of psychic healing and occult involvement. It also provides basic training in Christian theology, jargon and methodology — enough, in fact, to enable one of its graduates to infiltrate and take over a Christian congregation unrecognized. That was what Will Baron was there for.

Infiltrating Christian congregations

Back in California Baron had begun to channel another 'dead master', 'Jesus Christ'. The female guru who dominated the Lighted Way community had told him that he must channel 'Jesus Christ' exclusively and, somewhat abashed, had admitted that Djwhal Khul had 'probably been Satan himself . . . '.

If Djwhal Khul had sought to control every aspect of Will's life, 'Jesus Christ' had all but made his life hell above ground. Often Will woke up at night to find himself being shaken. Sometimes the room shook, as if there was an earth-quake. His bed would tremble and, occasionally, revolve. His stomach would seem to turn on itself as if strong hands were twisting it. Pictures would sway on their mountings. Voices would be heard alternately cajoling and menacing.

The health problems which had originally taken Will to a New Age centre were uncured. Indeed, they were getting worse. Other ailments were manifesting themselves. All sorts of psychic healing techniques were used. Nothing worked. But there was always the hope. . . .

By now Baron and his female guru were having consider-able success channelling spirits they called 'the Father' and 'the Holy Spirit', as well as 'Jesus Christ'. Will was 'speaking in tongues', a gift he found of considerable value in gaining him access to certain Christian congregations, as well as a standing within them. Will introduced Christian congregations to his meditation techniques and, from there, sought to lead them into the occult world of New Age.

Soon he was 'preaching' his 'gospel', both from pulpits and in the open air. He convinced himself he was a 'Spirit-filled, New Age, born-again Christian'. So successful was Baron's infiltration of Christian congregations in California that the 'Jesus' spirit sent him on a third visit to Findhorn. Baron writes, 'My colleagues at Findhorn were surprised and bewildered by my statements declaring that I was a follower of "Jesus Christ", the only "Son of God", and "Lord" of all New Age masters. Faced with their astonishment I did not push the issue, concluding that they simply were not ready for the "revelation knowledge" I was privy to.'[5]

Not long after, once again, Baron had returned to the USA. He had another night-time visitation from the 'Jesus' spirit. It said, 'I am coming soon. You have got to do my work. Time is running out.' From now on Baron began to ex-pect and preach the imminent, esoteric though physical ap-pearance of Jesus Christ.

He redoubled his preaching efforts. He found to his amusement that popular clergymen — including televangelists — were both using New Age jargon and telling their followers imminently to expect Jesus Christ to walk down the aisles of their congregation. . . .

The rescue

Even at the height of his success, Will told me, his 'spiritual life' went seriously sour. His familiar spirit had nothing but anger and threats for him. He felt tormented. He repeatedly received impulses to commit hari-kari with a sharp knife. His rages became uncontrollable. Believing that the 'Jesus' he channelled was the real thing he repeatedly blasphemed the name of Jesus Christ.[6] To his surprise the spirits never showed any anger or punished him for his blasphemy.

'What I call my "rescue" came about as a result of reading Christian books,' Will Baron told me. 'And these Christian books led me to the biblical book of Revelation. . . .'

While channelling was sweeping America and becoming big business[7] Will Baron had praying parents back home in Lancashire. While attending a Gospel rally Will found someone else to pray for him. The evangelist had preached straight Gospel. There was not a hint of New Age about the whole campaign. A woman in her mid-30s asked him what kind of Christian he was. Will had dropped his guard. The spirits had always been insistent that he should never tell anyone of his New Age affiliation. On this occasion he blurted out, 'I am a New Age Christian.' On the spot the woman began to pray for him — aloud.

Will discovered the New Testament. He found Revelation gripping. He read of an end-time power — Antichrist — that would seek to deceive and destroy God's true followers and masquerade as Christ. He would perform 'great and miraculous signs' and 'because of the signs' would deceive 'the inhabitants of the earth'.[8]

Will was in agonies. Djwhal Khul, 'Jesus Christ', the masters, the hierarchy — what were they? What was the power behind it all? And, whatever that power was, why was it so important that Christian congregations should be infiltrated, seduced and undermined? The full occult horrors of New Age had not been unleashed upon him. But he now knew there *were* hideous shapes in the darkness. What *were* these shapes?[9]

Ultra-sceptical John Hick, after exhaustive research into psychic phenomena, was obliged to accept that 'deliberate fraud' could 'for all practical purposes' be excluded in the best cases of 'trancemediumship'. The view taken by Professor Hick is that while New Agers may not be channelling 'masters' who have been dead for thousands of years and, while mediums may not be communicating with the spirits of dead relatives and friends, 'something very strange is going on'.[10]

All of which begs an obvious question, What is it? And what power is behind it?

---

[1]This quote is taken from page 61 of Will Baron's *Deceived by the New Age: the Story of a New Age Priest* published in 1990 by Pacific Press. This is the most authentic exposé of the New Age and makes gripping reading. [2]Ibid, page 82; *The Sunday Times*, Scotland supplement, 2 August 1992. [3]See David Marshall, *The Devil Hides Out* (Autumn House 1991), pages 120-123. [4]*Close Encounters with the New Age* (Kingsway 1991) is an account of Kevin Logan's course and impressions of Findhorn. [5]Will Baron, op cit, page 136. [6]Ibid, pages 154-157. [7]John Drane, *What is the New Age Saying to the Church?* (Marshall Pickering 1991), pages 24-27. [8]Revelation 13:13, 14. [9]An idea of the extent of New Age infiltration of Christian congregations can be gained from *The Seduction of Christianity* (Harvest House 1985) by Dave Hunt and T. A. McMahon, and from Tony Higton's 'The New Age Meets its Match', *Christian Weekly*, 29 June 1990, page 6. Frank Hammond's two books, *Pigs in the Parlour* and *Demons and Deliverance* (New Wine Press 1991 and 1992) provide guidance for pastors who find that individuals within their congregations are suffering spirit infestation. [10]John Hick, *Death and Eternal Life* (MacMillan 1985), pages 130 *et seq.*

The Shapes in the Darkness

The occult world is dark. There are shapes in the darkness. What are they? Can we risk treading the darkness without knowing?

Will Baron had lived for years among the dark shapes. He had seen them, at first, as light and sources of light. But as, little by little, he came to embrace the Christian faith, the dark shapes emerged as the demon terrors they had always been. He was to discover the true identity, history and future of what the New Agers call 'the entities'. And he was to do so by discovering the Book and the Man in the Book: the Bible and its central figure, Jesus Christ, God's only Son who lived, died and conquered death through the resurrection. Will was to discover that through the *true* Jesus Christ every human has the offer of pardon, peace, purpose, salvation and eternal life. *In the Bible he found the baloney detector against which the unreason of New Age can be exposed and through which it can be confounded.*

It took many months for Will to make the transition between New Age priest and infiltrator of Christian congregations, to a true, Bible-believing, evangelical Christian. 'How did the "masters" and the "spirits" relate to that?' I asked him.

'They were enraged,' Will answered. 'The next few months were to be the most difficult of my whole life. The difficulties increased immensely when I began to write *Deceived by the New Age*. The heavy weight of depression seemed crushing and, again and again, while driving the car, a suicide impulse, almost too powerful to resist, came upon me. I owe my survival to the fact that the love and grace and power of God are broader than the measure of men's minds. But I can certainly understand what happened to Randall Baer. . . . Talking to those most closely associated with Baer, the form of Christianity he adopted was experiential rather than biblical. Perhaps the seeds of his suicide were in this; you need to meet the devil with a "Thus saith the Lord".'

I asked Will Baron that if he had to crystallize in a few words the danger posed by the New Age movement, what would those words be.

He answered; 'The principal danger? Demonic control through Eastern meditation techniques of men and, through men, demonic control of the world.'

International hoax

In the course of his transition Will experienced many violent shocks. He was in agonies when he realized that Djwhal Khul and even the spirits which had identified themselves as 'the Father', 'Jesus Christ' and 'the Holy Spirit' had been Satan's evil angels. For years he had allowed demons to mainline into his mind. The demons had been part of a world-wide movement to counterfeit Christianity. They had sought to use him as part of a great, international hoax. 'I suddenly understood that Satan is ultimately preparing the world for his spectacular appearance', writes Will, 'in which millions and millions of people will proclaim him to be Christ the returned Messiah. In reality it will be the appearance of the antichrist.'

Where evil began

Satan and his demons had been training him as a false prophet. The 'masters of the hierarchy' had been demons masquerading as agents of God. He read Revelation 12 and, in verses 7-9, found the record of a civil war which had taken place in heaven before the creation of the world; and in verse 4 he found the implication that one third of the angelic host had rebelled with Lucifer (Satan) and had been expelled from heaven. These fallen angels had become demons; and these demons had been his constant companions for some twelve years and he, their slave.

Will Baron found a proper understanding of Revelation 12 to be the key in exposing the whole masquerade of the psychic.

The shapes in the darkness were angels-turned-demons; 'the spirits of devils, working miracles'. Revelation 16:14. He reflected that the New Age was to be brought about by co-operation between channellers ('enlightened ones') and 'extraterrestrials' who were already on the planet. He shuddered. The ETs with which New Agers communicated, and on which the success of their cause depended, were demons.

Will found that Jesus had prophesied that in the age before His return there would be counterfeit, esoteric 'returns'. He found, too, that Jesus had given specific instructions that His followers were to stay away from the false (Matthew 24:4, 5, 11, 23-27).

Will Baron burned a mountain of esoteric literature he had used during his years as a New Age priest. However, in some of the books he burned, he would have found quotations in which mediums/channellers acknowledged the possibility/likelihood that the 'entities' with which they communicated and which communicated through them were evil spirits.

Medium Brenda Crenshaw warned that 'there are spirits . . . who are willing to come back to a medium and take possession of him with a view to manipulating him as a channel of evil to the world'. Veteran New Ager Ruth Montgomery warned that channelling was potentially 'opening a door through which mischievous and malevolent spirits might enter' and that through spiritist seances and New Age channellers, the 'door' had been opened in Western lands to frightening possibilities.[1]

The baloney detector

Will Baron's discovery of the Bible gave him the foundation on which to stand, the yardstick with which to measure, and the lie detector to apply to New Age.

The great questions of life, death, time and eternity

are, he discovered, answered in this book of books.

Against the longest odds imaginable the discovery of ancient manuscripts in the last 150 years or so has demonstrated that its text has not been corrupted by time. Over the same period the findings of archaeologists have authenticated as fact the details of its narrative previously contested or, in some instances, laughed off as mythical.[2]

The manuscript evidence for the New Testament alone is far in excess of that for any other document of antiquity. There are 5,300 Greek manuscripts, 10,000 Latin Vulgate manuscripts and more than 9,300 manuscripts of other early versions. The next most authenticated work is Homer's *Iliad* for which 643 manuscripts survive. Further to this, in no other case is the time interval between the original work and the earliest extant manuscripts so brief as in the case of the New Testament. The Ryland Fragment, a part of John's gospel, dates from *circa* AD 120, approximately twenty years after the original was written by John.

Working with mature Christian pastors, Will Baron subjected the Bible to a most critical appraisal before accepting it as God's revelation to man. Once he had reached this point he realized that the manuscripts and the artefacts were merely evidences for faith. He found that the Bible was self-authenticating. He discovered that it was the sort of book that a man could not write if he would, and would not write if he could. The content of the Bible, he found, was such that men and women, by exposing themselves to it, could discover that it was inspired by God.

Like many great minds through the ages, Will came to believe that 'if they speak not according to this word, it is because there is no light in them'. Isaiah 8:20.

The Bible is the only baloney detector — yardstick of truth and exposer of error — available to man.

Food for the soul

Western man reacted against the radical materialism of

the 1980s because it did not fulfil his most fundamental longings, nor provide nourishment for the human spirit. Materialism had produced *rootlessness, aimlessness, lostness, loneliness* and *disintegration.*

And, dissatisfied with materialism, Western man had turned to New Age with its conflation of Eastern mysticism and the hardcore occult in his search for roots, aims, direction, fulfilment and stability. Only to find, like Will Baron, that New Age answered none of his questions and fulfilled none of his needs.

The *real* consequences of New Age becoming a mass movement were decidedly more sinister. Cut away the crust of baloney from New Age and, at its core, was old-fashioned occult activity barely distinguishable from spiritism and other ancient forms of the occult. New Age has also been a catalyst of a world-wide upsurge of all forms of occult activity, including witchcraft and Satanism. Among the spin-offs of this upsurge has been a quantum leap in the incidence of the ritual (satanic) abuse of children, and other forms of organized paedophilia. Impressive documentation — as well as detailed and convincing case studies and testimonies — of the horrifying growth of all forms of occultism has been provided in a whole variety of newspaper reports[3] and books,[4] including some that specifically address the horrendous upsurge of the ritual abuse of children.[5]

All this comes in the wake of the New Age movement that turns on so many of Hollywood's bright and beautiful.

By contrast, the Bible introduces its reader —

TO HIS ROOTS. Matter plus Time plus Chance do *not* make a world. Man, Matter and Time exist by divine fiat. Man was made in the image of an all-powerful, all-knowing, all-loving Creator God.

Christianity provides roots that anchor, nourish and explain a man. Intellectually, it provides him with roots that are a safeguard against every latest fad, fantasy and philosophy. Morally, it provides a strong and satisfying shelter in a code aimed to safeguard and maximize his happiness and that of those who are part of his family community, country and world. Emotionally, the Bible gives him roots that provide a sense of true belonging; that though a man may live and grow and journey and pass away — though the earth itself may be transitory, impermanent — he has roots among eternal things.

To HIS AIMS. Christianity brings with it purposeful living. The God who made man in His image loves him as an everlasting Father. Life *is* more than a dusty scuffle over a parched terrain between Point Birth and Point Death. Life *is* more than a catalogue of accidents. Life *is* more than a nightmare between two eternities. Life committed to God has purpose and aim, and both are tied up in a relationship of trust into which all comers are invited.

In a universe too big to measure, in which the earth is a mere speck of stardust covered with countless millions each with his hopes, loves, dreams, loyalties and fears, the Bible emphasizes that every life counts and is of infinite value to the all-loving Father God.

Jesus knew how a pointless existence left the soul of man, like an empty house, prey to invasion by devils of all kinds, mischief, despondency, bitterness, despair. That's why he often stopped to talk to individuals and deliberately invited Himself to dine with those considered outcasts. We hear Him talk about the hairs of each head being numbered, about the value of one soul being beyond all creatures, beyond all sacred institutions, beyond the value of all the world.

Behind all history lies God's will, behind all human society stands God's kingdom, awaiting perfect manifestation and final fulfilment. Jesus speaks of a great purpose into which each individual life may be fitted. He calls men away from the nets, desks, benches, kitchen sinks, consoles and VDUs of futility — to follow Him in a quest for a better world, a richer life, an eternal kingdom.

To LIFE'S DIRECTION. In the Christian Way there are landmarks and guideposts. There is authority. Amid the babble of contradictory voices, one great Voice sounds above all: the voice of God through Scripture. And Scripture provides a prophetic structure in which past, present and future are part of a whole, and that whole our salvation. No one who has encountered the Christ of Calvary is ever lost. And all of his life is aimed towards God's denouement.

TO HIS FULFILMENT. Materialism marginalizes and makes many lonely; the occult draws in the lonely, and destroys them. Jesus, by contrast, met the lonely with a call to fellowship — 'the fellowship of the Son of God's love'. He sought out the lonely: the woman coming to draw water, the blind man ducking and diving to avoid the crowds, the ostracized tax collector, the leper shunned by society, the one man left at the Pool of Bethesda, the guilt-ridden Peter. And Jesus promises, 'I will not leave you desolate.'

TO HIS STABILITY. Materialism and the psychic lead to disintegration. Christianity makes for stability and ultimate security. God's love is stronger than that of any parent. The God of the Bible gives no copper-bottomed guarantee that His children will not encounter problems and difficulties. What He *does* guarantee is that when the problems and difficulties come, He will walk by our side and give us strength. That He hurts when we hurt. That no hurt will come our way until it has been sieved through His love, grace and power. That when it strikes — even though some of our questions may remain unanswered until we meet Him face to face — it will be made to work in some way for our everlasting good.

TO FEAR-FREE LIVING. God is sovereign, all-powerful. The world is more like a ship than an iceberg. The iceberg cracks off from the polar ice-cap in a thunderous explosion. After that its course and destiny are subject to all kinds of uncertainties. A ship has a captain, a navigator, charts, maps, and navigational equipment. The God of the Bible is a Captain who says, 'Trust me regardless of the storms and I'll guide the vessel into an eternal harbour.

Examine my record as set out in the Book. Look at the events foretold years before they happened and how they came to pass. See how I have set out my scenario of the future. Trust me in the little things of Time; I am concerned with the details of your life. Trust me in the big things of Eternity; I want to guide you through the worst to the ultimate best.'

To GUILT-FREE LIVING. Neither the Bible nor the God revealed in its pages have any illusions about man. God made men and women perfect. On behalf of the rest of us, the first Adam gave in to the force of evil present on the planet. That force led man, with his consent, into depravity and corruption. The natural tendency of the human choice-mechanism is towards the worst, rather than the best. But the Bible tells us how, though eternal right must be maintained, eternal love found a way to save sinners through the second Adam, God's own Son. That God gives both sin-sorrow and forgiveness; both the impulse to desire the best (against man's own nature), and the new life that *is* the best (against man's own deserts).

To ULTIMATE HOPE. The Bible promises that a glorious new world — beyond the pain and injustice of the present — awaits those who enter the new life amid the sorrows and uncertainties of the now. This is its message. In an uncertain world the assurance of eternity is possible. In an evil-choked world forgiveness, acceptance and high-level living are possible. In a world of conflict it is possible to live with supernatural peace. In a world of heartbreak it is possible to have a joy of the sort that it is in no man's power to take from you.

God has opened the way through His Son, the second Adam. *Everything* is possible through trusting Him and establishing a day-by-day relationship with Him. *That* is the message of the Bible.

There is no need to fear the darkness, or the shapes in the darkness, when you have made your commitment to Christ. The message of the birth, life, death and resurrection of Jesus: The darkness is illuminated with the light of God. The devil is a beaten foe. There is no reason to fear him. Good *is* infinitely stronger than evil. God has triumphed. Eternity is assured.

And, in the meantime . . . ?

---

[1]Cited in David Marshall, *The Devil Hides Out* (Autumn House 1991), page 66. [2]See the author's *Battle for the Book* (Autumn House 1991). [3]Beatrix Campbell, 'Vortex of Evil', *New Statesman*, 5 October 1990, pages 12-14; *The Observer*, 16 September 1990; 16 February 1992; 10 March 1991; 17 March 1991; 23 February 1992; *Daily Mail*, 13 March 1990; *Western Morning News*, 22 July 1992; *Today*, 24 April 1991; *Radio Times*, 25-31 July 1992; Jonathan Mortimer, 'New Age: Big Business', *Christian Weekly*, 13 June 1990; Tim Lenton, 'Ritual Child Abuse', *Christian Weekly*, 15 March 1991; Rowena White, 'The Age of Aquarius', *Christian Weekly*, 18 May 1990; Kevin Logan, 'Hell and Heaven', and Robert Runcie and John Stott 'Defining New Age', *Christian Weekly*, 25 May 1990; Rachel Downey, 'Porn is the Theory', *Social Work Today*, 28 February 1991, page 9. See also *The Devil Hides Out*, pages 38-43. [4]See Josh McDowell and Don Stewart's two books, *The Occult* and *The Deceivers* (both published by Scripture Press in 1992); Kenneth Wade, *Savage Future: The Sinister Side of New Age* (Autumn House 1991); Roy and Rae Livesey, *New Age to New Birth* (New Wine Press 1986); Kevin Logan, *Paganism and the Occult* (Kingsway 1988); Russell Chandler, *Understanding the New Age* (Word 1988); Russ Parker, *The Occult: Deliverance from Evil* (IVP 1989); Roger Ellis, *The Occult and Young People* (Kingsway 1989); Peter Wagner and Douglas Pennoyer (eds), *Wrestling with Dark Angels* (Monarch 1990). Guidance with regard to withdrawing from all forms of spiritual abuse is contained in David Johnson and Jeff VanVonderen, *The Subtle Power of Spiritual Abuse* (Bethany House 1991). [5]See Diane Core's *Chasing Satan* (Gunter Books 1991), a heart-rending, at times bilious-making, detailed account of her work with Childwatch to uncover the satanic sexual abuse of children in Britain; Audrey Harper's account of her involvement in witchcraft and paedophile rings in England in *Dance with the Devil* (Kingsway 1990) for which Member of Parliament Geoffrey Dickens has written a Foreword; Pat Palling's *The Devil's Web* (Word 1990) demonstrates how children are introduced to abuse and occult activity by games readily available in the shops; and Neil Anderson and Steve Russo's examination of the wider correlation between the occult and the abuse of children in the USA in *The Seduction of Our Children* (Harvest House 1991). The last-named book also gives guidance to the abused and to parents of abused children, as well as sound advice on safeguarding children against mental and physical abuse occasioned by New Age and the occult.

New Age and the New Fascism

And, in the meantime, it would appear that we have a fight on our hands.

The New Age menace to the world, society and the Christian Church, says Russell Chandler, Religion writer of the *Los Angeles Times*, 'will crescendo to a fever pitch' as 2000 approaches. 'The movement's major drawing power, according to Berkeley sociologist Robert Bellah . . . comes from the younger ranks of the well-educated middle class.'[1] Dr. John Drane anticipates the same New Age crescendo in Britain.

But Dr. Drane had to visit the USA to be made aware of the political menace represented by New Age. Part of a mass audience before which J. Z. Knight claimed to channel a 35,000-year-old warrior, Ramtha, the Scottish academic became aware of messiah-hunger. For twenty-five years British New Age leader Benjamin Creme has been seeking to feed this messiah-hunger with the message of a one-world government with a one-world leader. He believes that the UN is a 'conditioning device' in preparation for the world government to come. And, as every issue of his periodical *The Emergence* trumpets, the new World Leader will be a combination of the Christ looked for by Christians, the Messiah looked for by Jews, the Krishna looked for by Hindus, the new Buddha looked for by Buddhists and the Imam Mahdi looked for by Muslims. This great World Leader, says Creme, who will both usher in and personify the Age of Aquarius, the New Age, will be the Lord Maitreya.

As Creme goes on to expand his political ideas it becomes clear that what he is working for is a new, world-scale Fascism.

And this is what has Dave Hunt and Caryl Matriciana,

for years full-time New Age watchers, seriously worried.

Caryl Matriciana says, 'Creme's christ will not be the world teacher and ruler of world peace others are forecasting. Without question the stage is being set for the final apostasy prophesied in Scripture. The way is being prepared for the final actor, the counterfeit the Bible predicts who must come before the return of Jesus, the true Prince of Peace.

'Today's revival of paganism and Hindu practices which form the heart of the New Age movement has the same kind of foundation that prepared the way for Hitler's rise to power. . . .'[2]

The Germany of the 20s and 30s, in social and economic despair, looked for a messiah, *any* messiah. A whole society was in stress. The most comprehensive symptom of this exceptional situation of stress was the loss of a frame of reference for behaviour. The collapse of old institutions followed by a relatively long period of instability, weakened and destroyed in many individuals the sense of discrimination and orientation in social life. Nothing was unshaken and nothing unshakeable. People oscillated between a state of *naïveté* and one of desperate incredulity — all opinions equally good, equally meaningless.

Out of this national psychosis emerged Nazism and Adolf Hitler.

The same exceptional situation of stress, the same symptoms — the loss of a frame of reference for behaviour — exist in Western societies today.

Benjamin Creme claims to have a solution in a New World Leader who is, even now, 'waiting in the wings': the Lord Maitreya.

Beyond the New Age political agenda: a New Fascism.

So, on the cusp of the millennia, the New Age movement menaces democracy. The New World Order under the New World Leader will extinguish personal liberties. The triumph of Hinduism (or New Age) would mean a complete alteration in our concept of man, our traditions of democracy and humanitarianism; our social systems. All would become meaningless because they are built on Christian pre-suppositions.

According to New Age propaganda, before it can be ushered in it must first destroy its main ideological challenger: the Christian faith.

Whether an attempt is to be made to destroy the Gospel by force, or whether it is merely to be opposed by a seductive ideology of unreason, Christians have a fight on their hands.

How should Christians respond to this challenge?

Age of gullibility

Satan has prepared our age very carefully for a great deception. Gullibility is an essential part of his plan. And our age is nothing if not gullible.

Once Christians saw scientific scepticism as the enemy. Now most of us would settle for a bit of good, healthy, scientific scepticism. But the public mood is drop-jawed credulity. Give the most preposterous set of ideas the backing of a multi-million-pound public relations campaign and it is assured of a mass following.

In this age of gullibility New Age has given us 'false christs and false prophets' by the number. 'Signs and lying wonders', not to mention 'strong delusions' are on every hand. And everywhere Satan's 'angel of light' image is evident.[3]

The Elijah method

Satan had prepared Elijah's age for a great deception too. His preparation had begun with Ahab's marriage to Jezebel, a pagan princess.

But Jezebel was not just a pagan, she was a fanatical pagan: a priestess of Baal. With ruthless missionary zeal she began to spread this fertility cult throughout Israel. Ahab was led to worship Baal. A temple to Baal was built in the capital of the northern kingdom. Jezebel then commenced a campaign of compulsory evangelization, executing the prophets of Yahweh, and importing vast numbers of prophets of Baal from Sidon.

It wasn't that Israel *abandoned* the worship of Yahweh. There was still a *nominal* allegiance to the true God. What happened was that the worship of Yahweh and the worship of Baal were being hybridized together. It was typical New Age: 'the universe of faiths'; 'forget the creed, just enjoy the experience'.

Sometimes they worshipped Yahweh, sometimes Baal. Most of the time they couldn't remember who they were worshipping. To use Elijah's phrase, 'they wavered between two opinions' (1 Kings 18:21, NIV). Nowadays, of course, modern man wavers not just between *two* opinions, but several dozen. All voiced by scholars, all given prime-time TV, all taught in schools under the heading 'religion', and all well represented in the bookshops and video stores.

How are Christians responding to this state of affairs? In much the same way as the people did in Elijah's generation.

✧ In Elijah's story we encounter a character called Obadiah (1 Kings 18:3, 4). Obadiah had been a servant of Yahweh. Indeed, he had gone so far as to hide and feed 100 prophets from Jezebel's axemen. But he had become a collaborator with Ahab. And what had begun as collaboration ended with compromise. This is clear in Elijah's mode of address to Obadiah; 'Go tell your *master* . . .' (verse 8). Obadiah's response (verse 9) reveals the substance of the man; he had a yellow streak so broad you could rent space on it. As far as Obadiah was concerned, Elijah was far too dangerous a character for him to get mixed up with. Obadiah was used to playing safe; backing off from what was remotely radical or strident, let alone militant.

Obadiah's equivalent these days is the undercover Christian. When anti-New Age Christian evangelist Steve Russo went to Sedona — a place stuffed with New Age centres and bookshops; a sort of US Findhorn equivalent — he saw a Christian church. With some difficulty he secured an interview with the pastor. 'What's it like to pastor a church in a New Age centre like Sedona?' he enquired. The minister looked bewildered and replied, 'I don't know what you're talking about. There really isn't a problem here.'

Russo rephrased his question. 'With Sedona being a hot-spot for New Age activity, what challenges have you faced trying to minister in this city?'

The clergyman's reply shocked Russo. 'Young man, I learned a valuable lesson when I began my ministry. If you don't go looking for trouble, you won't find it.'

'Unfortunately this pastor's head-in-the-sand cop-out is all too characteristic of the church today . . . ', writes Russo.[4] Many Christians still need convincing that if you ignore New Age it really will *not* go away. . . .

But the Obadiah 'under-cover' reaction was only the first of three responses to the menace in Elijah's story.

✧ The second was from the 100 prophets hiding in the caves (verse 13). One scholar suggests that they were the 'schools of the prophets', thriving theological seminaries representing uncompromising enthusiasm for the cause of Yahweh. Jezebel certainly saw them as a menace to her campaign to impose Baal worship. But their response to the crisis was to withdraw into a secret society, retreat into a sphere of private religion. But you can't be a prophet in a cave, because a prophet is a mouthpiece. On two occasions (chapters 18:22; 19:10) Elijah made it clear that prophets in caves counted for nothing.

In face of the New Age menace many contemporary Christians fall under the same censure. They are godly men and women, no compromise about them, but they are so intimidated by the world that they have abandoned it, retreating into pious ghettos, a Christian sub-culture, safe from contamination. They talk a lot about holiness, but there is no prophetic edge to their witness. They talk a lot to one another but have nothing to say to the world.

✧ The third response to the crisis in Elijah's day was that of Elijah himself. As far as he was concerned this was no time for compromise or withdrawal. First, he made sure he understood the issues at stake and that he, personally, was fully committed to the cause of truth. Second, he engaged the enemy. This drought, he told Ahab, has nothing to do with the greenhouse effect — it's your fault! (See verse 17.) Then, having confronted the king, he engaged the representatives of the rival faiths (verses 19, 20 *et seq.*). This confrontation could almost be figurative of the final confrontation between good and evil. If we count the prophets of Asherah, as well as those of Baal, Elijah was outnumbered 850 to 1. The great confrontation was on Mount Carmel. There is now a vast monument where it took place!

In addition to numbers, Elijah knew that he was up against it in other ways. The sensual worship of Baal was far more appealing to fallen men and women than the lofty morality of Yahweh.

But Elijah knew that he had one major plus: his God was true. Good *is* stronger than evil. There were the altars to Baal with the false prophets screaming louder and louder, even slashing themselves with swords, screaming for Baal to send down fire to ignite their sacrifices.

Mid-day passed and they continued their frantic shrieking. Until the time came for the evening sacrifice. Baal had made no response. Satan was either impotent in the face of God's power, or he actually chose to let his followers down in their final confrontation. . . .

Don't miss this. The 101 pocket philosophies and occult religions on sale in the supermarket of our secular world are sham and lead ultimately to disillusionment, depression, mental illness and suicide. It is a fallacy that the devil looks after his own. He deserts, then destroys them.

Solid ground

The Christian stands on the solid ground of Scripture. In ten vital respects New Age teaching is the opposite of Bible teaching:

1. ABOUT GOD. New Agers take the 'god within' and 'god-is-in-everything' view.[5] The Bible makes a distinction

between the creature and the Creator. The God of the Bible is a personal, triune God.

2. ABOUT CHRIST. New Age teaches there are many 'christs' or 'masters'.[6] The Bible teaches that Jesus is the unique Son of God who came to earth to live, die and rise once and for all. It asserts powerfully that the only way to God and salvation is through Jesus Christ our Lord.

3. ABOUT THE ATONEMENT. The Bible has no truck with *karma*; it talks about *sin*. It asserts uncompromisingly that 'our great God and Saviour Jesus Christ' conquered sin, death and Satan by His perfect life, blameless death and glorious resurrection. It asserts that Christ is our righteousness; that in dying on the cross He made available to the repentant sinner forgiveness, and the covering of His perfect life of righteousness. Basic to New Testament theology is the substitutionary death of Christ; 'God made him who had no sin to be sin for us, so that in him we might become the righteousness of God.' 2 Corinthians 5:21, NIV. 'He was pierced for our transgressions, he was crushed for our iniquities; the punishment that brought us peace was upon him, and by his wounds we are healed.' Isaiah 53:5, NIV.

4. ABOUT MAN. 'It is the cardinal New Age teaching that man is born into this world both good and divine in his nature,' his salvation being dependent upon his 'looking inward' and 'recognizing that he is god'.[7] New Agers teach that man, unaided, has the power to be perfect and to make a perfect world. The Bible reveals man as helpless, powerless to do good, and that the only righteousness that can save him is the righteousness of the perfect Son of God. (See Matthew 9:13; Romans 3:10, 23; 1 John 1:9; 1 John 5:17; 1 Peter 3:18.)

5. ABOUT DEATH. New Agers teach there is no death, just a perpetual cycle of reincarnation. New Agers believe that there are dark realms of shadows from which the spirits of the dead can be summoned by a medium or channeller. To Bible-believing Christians the assertion

'there is no death' is the 'primal lie'; there is no shadowy realm of the spirit and 'mediums are an abomination'.[8]

6. ABOUT SIN AND JUDGEMENT. New Agers replace sin and judgement with karma, reincarnation and Nirvana. Fundamental to an understanding of the Bible is the sinful nature of man, and 'the Day of God' when all will be judged. The issue in the judgement? Their relationship with Jesus Christ. (See John 3; John 5:29; Revelation 20:10; 1 Corinthians 15:42-52; 1 Thessalonians 4:16, 17.)[9]

7. ABOUT THE WORLD. In the Bible there is no trace of the New Age monistic (all is one) or pantheistic (all is God) view. To the Christian these views detract from the sacredness of human life.[10] And conflict with their most fundamental belief: their view of God.

8. ABOUT THE FUTURE. New Agers believe that a 'global transformation' will be brought about by channellers (psychics) working in co-operation with 'extraterrestrials'. By contrast, the Bible anticipates a scenario in which life on earth deteriorates in an end-time age immediately prior to the second coming of Jesus Christ. The idea of a second coming, on average, occurs once in every twenty-five New Testament verses. In the Olivet sermon of Jesus (recorded in Matthew 24, Mark 13 and Luke 21) conditions prior to the second advent are described and the nature of the advent made clear. Paul rejoiced in the 'blessed hope' of Christ's appearance as King of kings and Lord of lords (1 Thessalonians 4:13-17), John records Christ's promise to return as the great hope for the world (John 14:1-3) and then, in his book of Revelation, describes the earth in its death throes, the second coming, and the kingdom to come after, in glorious technicolour.

In recent years evangelical Anglicans like John Stott, David Watson and Richard Bewes have been preaching the glorious return. In a recent book John Stott cites the words of Jesus to emphasize Jesus' 'belief that His coming would be a global, divine and cataclysmic climax to history, not a localized happening'.[11]

For the Christian the future is bright with promise.

9. ABOUT DEMONS. Some New Agers teach that there is no devil; others that he is a good angel given a bad press in the Bible. The Bible reveals Satan as the originator of evil and the enemy of all who want to live right.[12]

10. ABOUT TRUTH. New Agers teach that there is no such thing as absolute truth. The Bible reveals Jesus as 'the way, the truth and the life'. It records Jesus' promise that 'you will know the truth, and the truth will set you free' (John 8:32). Bondage to the spirits is the aim of New Age teaching. The freedom of the Gospel is the message of Christianity.

The key to Elijah's method and message was challenge (1 Kings 18:21): 'How long will you waver between two opinions?' Baal and Yahweh are not alternative routes to the same religious experience. They are routes in opposite directions. You will do the splits if you try to follow both.

No, says Elijah, all must choose.

As with Elijah the choice is still between a God who will hear and a god who is (for all practical purposes) deaf to the needs of his followers; a God who will act and a god who is impotent; a God who is true and a god who is false.

After the last great confrontation the entire universe will echo with praise for a single name: 'Every knee shall bow in heaven and in earth; and every tongue confess that Jesus Christ is Lord.' (See Philippians 2:10, 11.)

The crisis is upon us. The last great deception has arrived. It is not time for compromise. It is not time for withdrawal into private religion. It is time, first, to grasp the issues and renew our commitment to the Gospel and, second, to engage and confront.

But there will be no engaging or confronting until we grasp, live, breathe the Gospel. . . .

---

[1]Russell Chandler, *Understanding the New Age* (Word 1989), pages 24, 25.
[2]John Drane, *What is the New Age Saying to the Church?* (Marshall Pickering

), pages 24-27, 84-86, 107, 108; *Gods of the New Age*, video, (Riverside Films, 1984), Part 2. [3]See the prophecies of Jesus in His Olivet sermon (Matthew 24, Mark 13, Luke 21), and see the prophecies of Paul in 2 Thessalonians 2 and 2 Corinthians 11. [4]Neil Anderson and Steve Russo, *The Seduction of our Children: Protecting Kids from Satanism, New Age and the Occult* (Harvest House 1991), pages 47, 48. [5]For concise summaries of New Age beliefs see Josh McDowell and Don Stewart, *The Deceivers* (Scripture Press 1992), pages 219-246. [6]See Josh McDowell and Don Stewart, *The Occult: The Authority of the Believer over the Powers of Darkness* (Scripture Press 1992), pages 75-128. [7]Walter Martin, *The New Age Cult* (Bethany House 1989), page 39. [8]Deuteronomy 18:9-14; 1 John 4:1; John 11:11-24; 1 Thessalonians 4:13-17; John 5:28, 29; Psalm 115:17; Psalm 146:3, 4; Ecclesiastes 9:5, 6; Job 7:9, 10. See H. J. Berry, *The New Age Movement* (BTB 1988), pages 16-19, 26-34; John Stott, *Essentials* (Hodder and Stoughton 1988), pages 306-331; Michael Green, *I Believe in Satan's Downfall* (Hodder and Stoughton 1981). [9]Will Baron, *Deceived by the New Age: The Story of a New Age Priest* (Pacific Press 1990), pages 123, 124. [10] Kenneth Wade, *Savage Future: The Sinister Side of New Age* (Review and Herald 1991). [11]John Stott, *Essentials*, page 309. See Walter Martin, op cit, pages 44-46. [12]See Walter Martin, pages 41-44; Michael Green, op cit.

The Greatest Power in the Universe

Christians will make no headway against New Age unless they know God.

Too obvious to be worth saying? Elementary, my dear Wassername?

Hardly. A two-minute conversation with many 'Christians' will be enough to tell you they have never encountered the God revealed in Scripture.

Some are scared of the consequences of such an encounter; prefer a compromised life in which 'church' fits into a once-a-week corner. Properly understood, this is 'churchianity', not Christianity.

Some are cultists. My definition of a cultist? Somebody who has a grasp of Christian theology but who has never allowed that theology to affect — let alone revolutionize — his life.

A third group are on a performance kick. They think they've got to get to God's kingdom by dint of hard slog. They feel they have to *deserve* salvation. They are holding out against God's grace. This is legalistic Christianity.

Churchianity, cultism and *legalism* are three common perversions of the Christian faith. The three groups have at least one thing in common; their experience (if they have one at all) is one-dimensional and does not tap into the power of God. Paul told Timothy that there would be such people in the end-time Church. First, he listed the symptoms of godlessness 'in the last days'; love of self, love of money, arrogance, ingratitude, lovelessness, violence and hedonism among them. Then, having listed the side effects of godlessness in the last days, Paul identified a 'form of godliness' that would afflict the Church. Some would adhere to the forms, but would seek to live without — and would therefore deny — the power of God. 'Have

Galatians – preach
justification by faith
not works

nothing to do with them,' Paul advised before going on to detail the ways in which they represented a menace to true Christianity. 2 Timothy 3:1-9, NIV.

To call yourself a Christian and at the same time deny God's power, renders you very vulnerable in the face of the New Age menace. You are certainly in no position to engage or confront it.

All these perversions of Christianity grow out of not knowing God.

New Age conspiracy?

It grieves me that some Christians actually engaged in confronting New Age in pulpit or print do not appear to know God. I draw this conclusion from the fact that they present a terrifying picture of the New Age menace that leads their hearers/readers to suspect that evil is stronger than good — and that God hasn't much of a future! Of course, they don't set out deliberately to give that impression. That's just what comes over. Their central emphasis is on the machinations of Satan and the ubiquity of demonic possession. For them the only way to salvation seems to be exorcism, instead of repentance and pardon.

A variant on this view is the conspiracy theory. Conspiracy theorists have New Age infiltrators in every congregation and believe that a secret international hierarchy of New Age activists has undermined every Christian denomination, every government and every major corporation, and is ready to take over the world when the word is given.

There *is* a New Age hierarchy. But this hierarchy is not headed by some guru and staffed by corporation executives. Indeed, it's not headed or staffed by humans at all.[1] At its head is the one who makes it his business to work against God and goodness; the originator of sin and rebellion.[2] The New Age movement has no visible structured leadership of human beings, nor have I found the slightest hint to suggest the existence of a secret human leadership network. The New Age operation is too haphazard. Devilry of all kinds demeans, renders demented, drives to suicide, destroys those who get involved. For a brief time they may have the illusion of power, but it is only an illusion. This will, doubtless, be true of Creme's Maitreya-under-wraps, whenever he emerges into daylight.

Christians who subscribe to the conspiracy theory with regard to New Age generate fear and defeatism. They have everyone checking over their shoulders, under their beds and in their closets — for demons. I have known Christians of mature *years* — though not *experience* — who, having sweated through the latest horror story from the religious press, start reading significance into every news item, nightmare and noise-off. Such Christians underestimate their God. As J. B. Phillips put it; 'Your God is too small.' What kind of a God would allow the devil to torment His own faithful followers with terrors from the devil's nightmare dimension? God is too loving, too gracious, too powerful to allow the devil to unleash his terrors on those committed to the cause of Christ.

Where demons have entered homes and lives, it is because individuals have exercised their freedom of choice and dabbled in the devil's domain. I have never encountered a single case of paranormal/occult phenomena unless the victim has, in effect, issued a formal invitation to the devil by flirting on the fringes of his demesne. Dabbling may, of course, take many forms. It may be ouija, or tarot, or the obeah, or crystals, or 'meditation', or absorption with astrology, or seances, or any one of a number of occult games, or witchcraft, or Satanism. Issue an invitation to the devil and — depend on it — he will respond! However, unless you have done so, God has drawn a line of defence which He will not permit demons to cross.

All of which brings us back to the point where we started.

Knowing God.

And the first thing we need to know *about* God is that He is love.

Grasp that and you will begin to *experience* divine love. When that happens you are opening your heart to the Gospel.

Lonely Hearts

The free newspaper they push through my letter-box has a large — and growing — 'Lonely Hearts' section. Recently one love-plea caught my attention: 'Yucky lady with dowdy hair, pimply complexion and horrible children, seeks awful man to love her.' Dateline has 35,000 'lonely hearts' in its computer.

Everyone looks for love. But what *is* love? The first definition in the Oxford dictionary: 'A term used in tennis.'

The Bible declares that God is the personification of love.[3]

Glimpses into the heart of God

The Bible seeks to give us glimpses into the loving heart of our all-powerful Father God.

◇ Isaiah compared God's love with a mother's love. Could a mother forget her baby? Could she ever turn her back on her child. But, says Isaiah, <u>God's love is even stronger</u>; '<u>Though she may forget, I will not forget you!</u>'[4] Isaiah 49 v 15

◇ 'It was not with perishable things such as silver or gold that you were redeemed. . . ,' wrote Peter. And, as I read those words, I am back in the Wilberforce Museum in Hull looking at the impedimenta of slavery. There is the auction block and, in my mind's eye, I am standing upon it. I can hear the mocking voices of the crowd. And the voices of the people who are bidding for my life. One stronger voice outbids the others. <u>He buys me</u>. *<u>And then he sets me free</u>*. The currency he uses is not perishable. He bought me 'with the precious blood of Christ'.[5]

◇ 'I am the Good Shepherd,' said Jesus. 'The Good Shepherd lays down his life for the sheep.'[6] 'Suppose one of you has a hundred sheep and loses one of them,' Jesus said in one of the parables intended to give us an insight into His Father's heart. 'Does he not leave the ninety-nine in the open country and go after the lost sheep until he finds it?'[7] The shepherd searches through the night in the briars and thorns of the wilderness crags until he finds the one lost sheep.

Cliff Richard has written, 'If God's love is true, it is the most radical, urgent good news ever delivered. *Personally I believe it.*'

✧ It has been suggested that the 'prodigal son' story should really be called 'The Parable of the Father's Heart'. <u>Read it in Luke 15:11-24.</u>

It must have taken real bullet-proof insensitivity for this younger son to demand his share of inheritance from his father. It meant he'd been wishing his father dead.

In the Far Country he wasted a hard-earned fortune on instant pleasure. He paced the fastest set in town. This was life in the fast lane. But even a fortune runs out sooner or later. And in the Far Country the only law that seemed to prevail was the survival of the fittest. And that law says: When you've run out of fortune — stiff cheddar! That second son — once heir to a fortune — hit the pits: he was sent to work in a pigsty. There he was so hungry he found himself salivating when he looked at the contents of the trough. He reached a pragmatic decision: Even his father's servants ate better than this; he would go and ask his father to give him servant status in the home where once he had been a privileged son. He prepared a speech to impress his father.

In the event, the speech was never delivered.

Day by day his father had been peering into every dust cloud on the road from the Far Country for the familiar shape of his returning boy. So when the father saw him coming home he didn't wait for him to grovel, he ran out to meet him. Ignoring the stench of the pigsty, the father embraced the boy. When he kissed him he must have broken the boy's heart. In the pigsty he had made a practical decision. Now, seeing the depth of love in his father's heart, the boy realized just how wrong he had been and received the incentive to change. The father ordered 'the best robe' to be wrapped round his shoulders, shoes to be placed on his feet, a ring on his finger, and a party to be held in his honour.

The repentant son was not being given servant status. He was being received back as if he had never been away.

'This', Jesus was saying, 'is how my Father receives repentant sinners who want to return to the family home.'

If you're looking for love, you need look no further than our Father God. That fathomless love, represented in the words and the life and the death of Jesus, meets us at our point of need. 'Christ's love compels us,'[8] writes Paul, *2 Cor 5 v 14* and the Greek word translated 'compels' means 'gripped with a fever', 'surrounded as with an army'. That's how God's love is; gripping like a fever, surrounding like an army.

God's love is the most powerful force in the universe.

Understanding that transforms my life, gives meaning to my existence and keeps me safe from the terrors of the occult world.

The warnings of love

It is God's love that led Him to warn us against the 'detestable ways' and 'detestable practices' of occult involvement. It was His love that led Him to warn in such detail against mediums, spiritists, those who consult the dead, astrology — and every conceivable form of occult activity now practised in the New Age movement.[9]

'Dear Friends,' God pleads, 'Do not believe every spirit, but test the spirits to see whether they are from God. . . .'[10] *Apply the baloney detector.* A 'miracle' can be a fraud. That is not to say that mediums and channellers do not have a hot line to an unseen dimension. But, as we have seen, that unseen dimension has nothing to do with the dead and nothing to do with God.

Canon Michael Green was once 'invited to sign an open letter deploring the credulity of those who thought that demons still existed or were foolish enough to believe in a personal devil'. The Canon refused to sign; 'It seemed to me that the naïvety might possibly lie with those who wished so summarily to dispose of his Infernal Eminence.' Modern Christians, believes Green, are right to jettison the horns-and-hooves devil. Such a picture is unscriptural. But, says Green, the Bible 'very seriously warns us of a malign power of evil standing behind the pressures of a godless world without and a fallen nature within the Christian'.

This is how Canon Green sees it. There is a devil whose aim is to rebel against God and embroil the whole cosmos in his rebellion. He is the enemy of man, and a defeated enemy — the death blow having been delivered by Christ at Calvary. Nevertheless he continues to be very active and is never more pleased than when the idea of his existence is held in ridicule. He feels like a general who has persuaded the opposition to underestimate him. 'Doubt about the existence of a malign focus of evil is to be found,' writes Green, 'by and large, only in Christian lands.' Perhaps, if Satan were better known, he would be more hated, more resisted and more defeated in the lives of Christians.[11]

From Genesis to Revelation we encounter an anti-God force of great power and cunning. He is arrogant and determined, the implacable foe of God and man, who is out to spoil and mar all that is good and lovely. We find him in the Garden of Eden at the beginning of the story. We find him in the lake of fire at the Bible's end.

Jesus believed in Satan and had more to say about him than anyone else in Scripture. Satan is the one who tempted Him so skilfully and fiercely — as he tempts us — and who kept coming back at Him with devious suggestions all through His ministry. There could be no compromise with this evil force. Hence the cross. It sounded the death knell of the usurper. It was as He spoke of the cross that Jesus cried: 'Now shall the prince of this world be cast out. . . .'[12]

On the last night before Calvary, Jesus reiterated the

reality of Satan, "'The ruler of this world is coming. He has no power over me. . . .'"[13]

Where the aliens come from

Hollywood has now given us *The Alien, Aliens,* and *Alien III.* Sick and hideous as these films are, they do provide a metaphor for the beings that come from the devil's dimension.

Will Baron was right to find in <u>Revelation 12</u> the key to understanding the origin of evil.

Scholars believe that Isaiah's tirade against the king of Babylon in chapter 14 of his book is really a tirade against another and more sinister figure than the literal king of Babylon. (See verses 12-14.) The Isaiah passage clarifies the issue which originated Satan's rebellion.

Ezekiel (chapters 26-28) provides more background. The first ten verses of chapter 28 speak of the *prince* of Tyre, while the next nine speak of the *king* of Tyre. In Ezekiel's day Tyre was a prosperous and luxurious island kingdom lying to the north-west of Israel. When Ezekiel directs his message to the *prince* of Tyre he uses language appropriate to man. The language he directs to the *king* of Tyre is highly inappropriate to any man; it could not be used of any human being. Exactly the same spirit dominates the prince as the king. However, it is clear that when referring directly to the king, Ezekiel is speaking of Satan, and when referring to the prince he is referring to Satan's power and character demonstrated through man.[14]

Taken together the passages in <u>Revelation 12, Isaiah 14 and Ezekiel 28</u> answer the question: Who inhabits the unseen dimension of the spirit world, where did they come from and how did their evil nature originate?

There was an inter-galactic war — heaven's top angel officer — next to the Son of God — brilliant — intelligent — beautiful — but proud. Proud enough to challenge the authority of God's government. Lucifer (Satan) and his followers were cast out of heaven — and earth became the theatre of war.

Jesus Himself said, ' "I saw Satan fall like lightning from heaven." '[15] Jesus was recalling the great inter-galactic conflict back in the mists of pre-history and, in His mind's eye, recalling the fall of Satan and his hosts.

Who *are* the aliens who — when invited by occult dabblers — introduce terror into homes and lives?

They are angels turned demons — intelligent, observant, who, whether seen or unseen, have infested this planet for the thousands of years since the cosmic conflict began.

But remember: *God's love is the most powerful force in the universe.*

To be embraced by God's love is to be 'surrounded as with an army'.

Gomer came to God's love by the hard route. But, by doing so, she leaves us with an illustration that, no matter how sin-soaked, demon-dominated, hopeless our situation may seem to be, God has provided a door of escape. . . .

---

[1]Ephesians 6:12. [2]Ephesians 2:1, 2. [3]1 John 4:8. [4]Isaiah 49:15, 16 (first part), NIV. [5]1 Peter 1:18, 19, NIV. [6]John 10:11-18, NIV. [7]Luke 15:4, NIV. [8]2 Corinthians 5:14, NIV. [9]Deuteronomy 18:9-14, NIV. [10]1 John 4:1, NIV. [11]Michael Green, *I Believe in Satan's Downfall* (Hodder & Stoughton, 1981). [12]John 12:31. [13]John 14:30, RSV. [14]See especially Ezekiel 28:12-17. [15]Luke 10:18, RSV.

The Door of Hope

The climax of Gomer's story finds her on an auction block.

Auctions have always held a strange fascination for me. It's partly the auctioneer's patter, partly the weird and (very occasionally) wonderful articles offered for auction and, more than anything else, it's trying to work out why people are willing to pay what they *do* pay for the weirder and less wonderful articles.

The fascination dates from my school days. The auction rooms in the town where I went to school were conveniently near the station. On many occasions I have pushed my way into the crush of bodies to kill twenty minutes or so until it was time to catch the 5.14.

'What am I bid for this item which no household can afford to be without?' And there it was. Some kind of mechanical contraption with cogwheels, and handles, and prongs, and levers and springs.

'What is it?' I hollered from the back. There was a ripple of laughter. With my blue cap and my satchel I was a familiar figure.

'A question from Goliath at the back,' riposted the auctioneer. 'What is it? he wants to know. Well, I can't rightly tell. But if you had one already, this would make it a pair!'

This time a roar of laughter. And somebody bought it for fifty shillings.

I have seen folk, aglow with triumph, bearing away the most useless or the most hideous items from those auction rooms. What made them pay money far in excess of the apparent worth of the items purchased?

The value of a soul

Thomas Hardy commences his book *The Mayor of*

Casterbridge with the story of an auction with a difference. The story is based on a real-life happening. At a country fair in deepest Wessex, having imbibed more of the rum-laced furmity than was good for him, a young husband auctioned his wife. A sailor bought her. How much do you suppose he paid?

Five guineas.

In the terrible days of slavery men and women were auctioned to the highest bidder. When, after a fifty-three-year campaign by William Wilberforce, slavery was abolished in all British territories, the freed slaves sang, 'No more auction block for me!' In the Abolition of Slavery Act (1833) millions of pounds were made over by the British Government to the plantation owners to purchase the freedom of the slaves. When the aggregate sum was divided by the number of slaves freed, it worked out that the government had paid £37 per slave. That was the average market value of a slave in 1833.

What *is* the value of a soul?

A slave auction in a Middle East market. Prostitutes were for sale. And beery, red-faced men lolling on the fringes made free with blue, ribald remarks. The attractive women went first. Then raddled wenches who had seen hard usage. Finally, at last, one unfortunate woman remained unsold. She was worn out and haggard; years of low life had taken their toll. She'd once been in great demand. No one wanted her now. There was a faraway look in Gomer's eye. Was she too hard for tears? What was she thinking?

Once she had had a husband, a good man. Indeed, a prophet of God; Hosea. From the first, she had been unfaithful. And Hosea had had to live with the knowledge of her unfaithfulness.

She had left the family home. Hosea had to be mother and father to the three children, two of them probably not his.

Away from home, Gomer had descended to the depths of degradation. Eventually she even lost her freedom. She became the property of one lover after another. Then, at last, she was unwanted. Put up for auction. Right there in the centre of the community where everyone knew her story. And no one wanted to buy.

But wait.

Gomer's hard gaze settled on a figure, once familiar, purposefully shouldering his way through the crowd. What was he shouting? 'I'll take her! How much?' said Hosea. (The price of a slave was thirty pieces of silver then.)

'She's a special! Half price!' said the auctioneer. 'Fifteen pieces of silver and a homer and a half of barley, a day's ration. Can't say fairer than that.'

And Gomer was bought back by her husband.

Would you have done it? What *is* the value of a soul?

The suffering of God

Hosea filled the prophetic office in the northern kingdom for at least seventy years. It was the darkest age of Israel's unfaithfulness. So Hosea was uniquely fitted to discharge his office; he knew from bitter experience what it was like for God to love — and to meet no response.

Hosea developed a tremendous capacity to plead with the people, and an even more tremendous insight into the loving, wounded heart of God. He understood something of what God suffered when His people sinned. Israel — of which Ephraim was the dominant tribe — was playing the harlot. But God could not stop loving her. 'How can I give you up, Ephraim? How can I hand you over, Israel?'[1] Intermixed with pleading, God made a series of affirmations: 'I will not . . . I will not . . . I am God the holy One . . . I will not . . . I will not.' There is the language of tenderness and a promise of restoration; 'I will . . . make the Valley of Trouble a door of hope . . . .'[2]

Even in the Valley of Trouble, the pits of unfaithfulness, a door of hope. A shaft of light in the deepest darkness. A door that swings into the light of the Father's home and the warmth of the Father's heart.

God hates sin. It defeats the purpose of love. It reacts

to blight and blast and dwarf and damn an individual. But God loves the sinner and points to the door of hope: the Gospel. Over the rubbled remains of sin-ruined lives, God pleads; ' "Is it nothing to you, all you who pass by? Look around and see. Is any suffering like my suffering?" '[3]

'Do what I do'

And here is Hosea with his three children. He has not seen Gomer in years. And who would not say he was well shot of her? Not God. He gatecrashed Hosea's life. 'Go to Gomer. Buy her back. Restore her to your home. Love her *as the Lord loves his people.*'[4]

God still loves in spite of sin. He calls to the sinner in order to buy back, restore, renew, revive. It was as if He said to Hosea: 'Go, do what I do.'

Hosea was in the market place. Imagine Gomer's condition when he found her. How much did he pay for her? 'She's a special! Half price! Fifteen pieces of silver . . . .'[5]

And what now? The whole prophecy is the answer. The notes that thrill and throb and tremble like a paean of triumph. It was a case of: 'Rejoice with me, I have found the sheep that was lost.' The prodigal daughter of the Old Testament had come home.

Calvary

And, for myself, I am filled with wonder, and do not understand.

Until, that is, I come to Calvary.

The Gospel is gleaming in Hosea. But it is shining full-brilliant in Christ.

In my imagination, I see another auction. Not in a market place at midday, but in a garden of gnarled olive trees in the darkest of all midnights. Sweat drops of blood were upon Jesus as He pressed His face to the cold, hard ground. The collective weight of all the world's wickedness was on His shoulders and crushing the very life out of Him. There was the awful feeling of separation from His

Father. The agony of betrayal by a friend — for thirty pieces of silver, which at the then market rate was the cost of a down-market slave. There was the flight of His followers.

By actual experience He was beginning to taste death for everyone. A titanic struggle raged in His soul. Clinging to the hard ground, He said, 'Oh my Father, if it be possible, let this cup pass . . . .'

Then the most important word in the Book. '*Nevertheless* . . . . ' Nothing was inevitable about what happened in Gethsemane. The outcome of the auction had been prophesied but not predetermined. Would He wipe the blood-sweat from His brow and leave humanity, including you and me, to perish in our self-made cesspit? '*Nevertheless . . . your will be done.*'

When the priests and scribes and the temple guard, their blazing torches almost engulfed by the thunderous, unnatural darkness, entered the olive garden, the auction was over.

At the Place of the Skull next day the price was paid.

Agony and death; hideous, writhing, obscene. A vast crowd catcalling. Voices hissing with bitterness and aggression. Upturned faces, many contorted and grotesque with hate and scorn. Roman nails square in section in the wrists and the feet. A thorn crown crushed on His brow. The whole hideous instrument of torture and execution savagely jolted in the socket prepared for it in the rock face.

He was paying the price of a soul.

The worth of a soul can be estimated only by the price paid for its salvation: CALVARY.

Calvary: the door of hope.

His hands pierced for the wrong things our hands have done. His feet spiked for the wandering paths our feet have trod. His brow thorn-crushed for the wrong thoughts our minds have harboured. His side spear-riven to prove once and for all that the way to God's heart is wide open.

A strange transaction, this: His righteousness in exchange for our sins: and all made possible by God's great grace, through the faith He gives us.[6]

A strange transaction, but the heart, soul and centre of the Christian Gospel.

Give me *that* Gospel — not the endless wheel of karma and reincarnation.

The Christ of *that* Gospel redeems me and gives me freedom. The Lord Maitreya and the New Age philosophy cannot provide forgiveness and new life through new birth. It seeks to take away my freedom and fill my life with terrors. Jesus offers joy and peace. Maitreya holds out depression, suicide and everlasting bondage. No contest! Through the Door of Hope Jesus opened on Calvary shines everlasting life!

---

[1]Hosea 11:8, NIV. [2]Hosea 2:14, 15, NIV. See foot reference a. [3]Lamentations 1:12, NIV. [4]See Hosea 3:1 and G. Campbell Morgan, *Hosea: The Heart and Holiness of God* (Baker Book House 1974), pages 7-29. [5]Hosea 3:2. [6]2 Corinthians 5:21; Ephesians 2:8, 9.

When You Want Out

Because of Calvary there is deliverance from sin, and even from the dark and hideous world of the occult.

Those seeking this kind of release must accept certain truths. Tell them — and help them understand:

1. CHRIST IS YOUR ONLY HOPE. He is the only door to salvation. Acts 4:12. By committing your life to Him, you can cross over the line from death into life. John 5:24. Even in this world of perils and uncertainty you can know peace and assurance.

Unless you are prepared to surrender your whole life, body, mind and spirit, to Jesus Christ you will never find the peace and release you seek. Satan will try to attract you as an angel of light, and ultimately blow your mind with terror and destruction.

The awesome witness of the Bible is this: 'For this purpose the Son of God was manifested, that he might destroy the works of the devil.' 1 John 3:8. Jesus died that 'he might destroy him who holds the power of death — that is, the devil.' Hebrews 2:14, NIV.

Satan is subtle. He seeks to misrepresent, caricature Christians. He wants to produce hybrid Christians with warped personalities. He wants Christians to deny the power of their faith, to be sterile. By thus 'infiltrating' phonies into the Christian camp he can provide stumbling blocks to those who are perishing. He aims to rob Christians of the peace, joy and assurance that is their birthright. He wants to take away their freedom and destroy their relationship with the risen Jesus. That is why Christians are constantly warned to walk according to the light (1 John 1:6, 7); to be on the alert (1 Peter 5:8); to 'put on the full armour of God so that you can take your stand against the devil's schemes' (Ephesians 6:11, NIV).

2. YOU MUST ACKNOWLEDGE THAT EVERY INVOLVEMENT

WITH THE OCCULT IS, IN FACT, A PACT WITH THE DEVIL. It gives him a legal right to bind and oppress you. (Exodus 20:3-5.) There is only one way to shut the door on the devil: Come to Jesus Christ in confession and renunciation.

The occultists in Ephesus who turned to Jesus, 'came, confessing and divulging their practices' (Acts 19:18, RSV), renouncing the hidden things (2 Corinthians 4:2). Destroy occult objects (Acts 19:19).

Deliverance from demonic bondage is like our salvation. It is 'not of yourselves; it is the gift of God: not of works . . . ' (Ephesians 2:8, 9). It is not based on our merit. Not dependent on our feelings. Regardless of your emotional state at this point, you've come before God with an open heart in confession. Hence you have the assurance of 1 John 1:9 that He is 'faithful and just to forgive us our sins, and to cleanse us from all unrighteousness'. The door has now been shut on Satan. Don't let him take away your faith in this fact.

3. WE LIVE IN THE END-TIME. THE FALSE CHRISTS AND FALSE PROPHETS AND FALSE MIRACLES PROPHESIED IN THE NEW TESTAMENT ARE HERE.

The devil knows he's running out of time. Nevertheless, however furious, however subtle the warfare, the believer who clings in obedience and faith to Jesus *never* retreats in the face of the onslaught of demons.

Now, you must become an active warrior in the final conflict. Demons are in terror before the one who understands the victory and the power of the blood of Christ. *It is that blood that has dissolved Satan's power over us.* Make sure at all times that you are 'washed in the blood of the Lamb'.

'Then I heard a loud voice in heaven say: "Now has come the salvation and the power and the kingdom of our God, and the authority of his Christ. For the accuser of our brothers, who accuses them before our God day and night, has been hurled down. They overcame him by the blood of the Lamb and by the word of their testimony." ' Revelation 12:10, 11, NIV.

This is the greatest weapon God has given us: the protection of the blood of the Lamb that cleanses from all sin.

4. GOD HAS ARMOUR AND REQUIRES US TO WEAR IT. No warrior goes into battle with only parts of his equipment. You need 'the full armour of God so that you can take your stand against the devil's schemes . . . .' Ephesians 6:11, NIV.

Because 'our struggle is not against flesh and blood' but against 'the spiritual forces of evil' (Ephesians 6:12), the full armour of God is essential. Unless you wear *the belt of truth* your armour will not hold together. Unless you have put on the *breastplate of the righteousness of Christ* your heart can be pierced through with pride and self-righteousness. Unless your feet are shod with *the sturdy shoes of the Gospel of peace,* you can be thrown off balance by every stormy wind of doctrine that hits you. Unless you take up *the shield of faith*, Satan's flaming missiles of doubt and temptation will lodge deep in your flesh and burn you. You need *the helmet of salvation* to guard your mind and the sword of the Spirit which is the living Word of God.

Never underestimate the power of prayer and worship in your battle with the devil. Never underestimate God's power to defend those who have claimed His protection.

The devil is a beaten foe. He received a mortal wound in the battle fought on Calvary. The terror of the occult was robbed of its power by Calvary and an Empty Tomb was left as a monument to the victory. 'Christ is the conqueror over all the power of the enemy, and on the cross He inflicted such a crushing defeat on the devil that whenever His name is named in faith, Satan is bound to flee . . . . I have seen this time and time again in lives afflicted by demonic possession. The demons have to leave when commanded to do so in the name of the Victor. That theme of Christ the Conqueror is one of the major ways in which the cross is seen in the New Testament.'[1]

But Satan is like the Axis forces in Europe in the Second World War. The Normandy landings proved decisive for the outcome of the war. The final defeat of the Axis powers was inevitable. But the war went on. They refused to accept defeat. Sometimes a degree of success attended their struggle. Occasionally things looked favourable for them. But nothing could alter the fact that they were doomed. The ultimate Victory Day dawned in 1945.

That is how it is with Satan.

Revelation 12 and 13 present, at first glance, a chilling scenario. Before Christ returns in glory the devil will make one last stand. A final confrontation will take place. There God will be victorious.

The end of the devil and his followers is certain. It will be in a lake of fire. (Revelation 19:20; 20:10.) The picture in Revelation says Michael Green, 'denotes final and irreversible ruin and annihilation rather than endless torment'.

Nevertheless, the lake of fire will be the end of all devils and demons and those who have followed them.

The final word . . .

The price of your soul was paid on Calvary. By seeing the price paid for us, we have seen deep into the heart of God. And love has its response. 'Ephraim shall say, What have I to do any more with idols?' (Hosea 14:8.) Our response? How can I any longer play with the knife that slew my best Friend? How can I any longer have intercourse with the dark, shadowy world of evil? How can I any longer make sin a way of life?

No more auction block for me. For I was bought with a price. And *what* a price!

There was hope for the Lost Son. There was hope for Gomer. There is hope for you.

The Door of Hope was opened for you on Calvary. Now, cross the threshold from death into life.

'Michael Green, *I Believe in Satan's Downfall* (Hodder and Stoughton 1981).

Time's Last Syllable

Tomorrow, and tomorrow, and tomorrow,
Creeps in this petty pace from day to day,
To the last syllable of recorded time;
And all our yesterdays have lighted fools
The way to dusty death. Out, out, brief candle!
Life's but a walking shadow, a poor player
That struts and frets his hour upon the stage,
And then is heard no more: is a tale
Told by an idiot, full of sound and fury,
Signifying nothing.

Shakespeare's Macbeth reflects on the brevity and futility of life and the future: a future without Christ.

Tomorrow, and tomorrow, and tomorrow. . . .

Let's look at three tomorrows. . . .

The world's tomorrow

A wealthy man threw an expensive party on his vast estate. The party centred around an enormous swimming pool with a shark in it. Wild and reckless, the host challenged every male guest that if he could dive into the pool and swim across it, successfully evading the shark he would give him one half of his money, or one half of his estate, or the hand of his beautiful daughter in marriage.

Suddenly there was a splash. A man was seen swimming for all he was worth. With tremendous skill he evaded the shark and dragged himself out of the pool at the other side, out of breath and spluttering.

The host was amazed. He went over to the swimmer and said: 'Congratulations! I didn't think it could be done! But I'm a man of my word. Tell me, do you want one half of my money?'

Still trying to regain his breath, the man said, 'No.'

'Do you want one half of my estate?'

Puffing and panting, the man blurted, 'No.'

'Do you want the hand of my beautiful daughter in marriage?'

'No.'

'Then what do you want?'

'I want the answer to just one question: *Who pushed me in?*'

In the present-day world of fast currents and any number of sharks, we may wonder, 'Who pushed me in?'

Epochs, these days, last only moments. Current history is like a VCR stuck on fast-forward.

First there was Gorbachev and his glasnost and perestroika.

Then freedom spread through Eastern and Central Europe from Estonia to Albania — like a forest fire.

And since then the consequences of freedom; the revival of nationalistic urges and the consequent fragmentation of the old USSR, Czechoslovakia, Yugoslavia.

Germany is united again, and Chancellor Kohl and senior European Commissioners speak of a 'United States of Europe'.

The Middle East is restless. The Islamic revolution began in Iran. There has been evidence of nuclear and chemical weaponry in Iraq and Libya.

And the VCR is still stuck on fast-forward. No one can call freeze-frame.

The plot becomes hard to follow. It's all happening too rapidly. It's as if history has gone into overdrive.

And, on top of it all, scientists are saying that the earth is becoming uninhabitable: earth-warming, the greenhouse effect, acid rain, the destruction of the rain forests, the erosion of the ozone layer, hurricanes, high winds, high seas, encroaching shorelines, famines in Africa, unnatural weather conditions. . . .

And Western societies seem to be disintegrating; climbing crime statistics, the collapse of the family, the escalating number of runaways, grotesque sex murders, the increased incidence of the sexual abuse of children.

And, over it all, occult-New Age forces overspread the earth like a foul miasma threatening to engulf everything. Inextricably connected with it, black witchcraft and Satanism are growingly practised, not only on remote beaches and moorlands, but in the major cities, the yuppy suburbs. . . .

The future of the world does not look promising. The freedom euphoria has evaporated. Freedom itself seems to have destabilized parts of Europe. Too much change in too short a time?

Where will it all end?

When the eco-system goes phut?

Or is the destiny of the human race really in the hands of half a dozen men who work the political super-gladiators?

Are we at the mercy of the first terrorist group or maverick State to get its hand on nuclear weapons?

Or — worst case scenario — do we face the nightmare, New Age future in which demons shape our destinies, from which all moral restraints are removed? An age in which, in the words of John White, ' "Channelling" will be considered the norm rather than the exception,' everyone with his own 'spirit guide'.[1] The 'New World Order': the New Nazism of the gurus — and 'the Lord Maitreya'. 'The guruistic system of politics is very dangerous for our democratic society,' says German journalist Fritz Haack. 'It will at least bring a loss of freedom, a loss of security and a big danger for mankind. I believe that guruism (New Age) is preparing the world for neo-Fascism.'[2]

If, somewhere in there, is the shape of tomorrow, we have every right to ask, 'Who pushed me in?'

God's tomorrow

'What on earth is God doing, for heaven's sake?' A British Member of Parliament asked it, and it's a good question.

Elie Wiesel, a survivor of Auschwitz, tells the story of a boy whom the SS suspected of sabotage and who was hanged alongside two adults. The three victims were mounted together on three chairs, their necks placed in nooses. At a sign from the head of the camp the three chairs were tipped over. 'Long live liberty!' cried the two adults. The child was silent. '*Where is God? Where is He?*' somebody asked, behind Wiesel. There was total silence in the camp. The adults had died instantly, but the boy was too light. He remained alive for at least half an hour. From behind him, Wiesel heard the same man asking: 'Where is God now?' Within himself Wiesel answered: 'Where is He? Here He is — hanging on the gallows.'

So what then, of God's tomorrow? What of the future if there *is* a God unlimited?

What did Jesus say about closing time on planet earth?

During the week prior to His crucifixion, the disciples of Jesus came to Him privately asking (Matthew 24:3, RSV), ' "Tell us, . . . what will be the sign of your coming and of the close of the age?" '

The reply Jesus gave to this question is recorded in detail by three of the four gospel writers (Matthew 24; Mark 13; Luke 21).

So, then, these indicators of the 'end'. What were they?

FALSE CHRISTS AND FALSE PROPHETS. New Age has given us a plethora of both.

WARS AND REVOLUTIONS. These have been endemic since Jesus uttered these words. But in the century now coming to a close, there has been a difference. A difference of scale and of pace.

NATURAL DISASTERS. 'There will be famines and earthquakes in various places,' prophesied Jesus. 'All this is but the beginning of the birth pangs.' In today's world millions die every year because they're too hungry to stay alive. In the past century there have been more major earthquakes recorded than in the previous 1,900 years combined. Nor is this just a matter of more sophisticated recording equipment; historians and scientists have, over the centuries, kept tally of the major upheavals in the earth's crust. Only in the past few decades has the frequency shown such a staggering upturn.

INCREASED SUFFERING AND PERSECUTION. In this sophisticated century there have been more martyrdoms for Christ than in the rest of the history of the Christian Church put together.

THE TRIUMPH OF THE GOSPEL. The blessed hope of the return of Jesus Christ will, according to Jesus Himself, only be realized when 'this gospel of the kingdom' has been taken to all the world.

God *is* in control. He *has* done something about the evil that dominates the world. And has done it at enormous cost to Himself in the person of Jesus Christ.

Wiesel was correct when he said: 'God is there, hanging on the gallows.' *Not* because God is dead. But because God endured that hanging.

As we look to Jesus by faith, we see the Lamb slain, slain in every funeral procession, slain in every victim of every catastrophe (Ethiopia, Somalia, Sudan, wherever), slain in every nervous breakdown, slain in every new horror and catastrophe.

But, says Jesus, when evil and violence escalate, it is not time to despair: ' "Men's courage will fail completely as they realize what is threatening the world, for the very powers of heaven will be shaken. Then men will see the Son of Man coming in a cloud with great power and splendour! When these things begin to happen, look up, hold your heads high, for you will soon be free." '[3]

And this Coming is no hole-in-the-corner affair. It will be the most visual, and the noisiest event in human history. It will be unmistakable, unexpected and, by many, unwanted. It will occur at a time when men are saying, 'Peace and safety.'[4] And the indication is that it will be business as usual on the day He comes. . . .[5]

The world's tomorrow, uncertain and desperately gloomy. God's tomorrow? Totally certain. The day of the Lord.

Your tomorrow

Everything about your tomorrow depends upon your attitude towards Jesus Christ — today.

There are two appointments in your future that you must keep, and you can put neither of them into your diary. The first is either death or the second coming of Christ (whichever comes first). The second is judgement.

How you stand in the judgement will depend upon whether you know the Judge.

If 'we have been justified through faith, we have peace with God through our Lord Jesus Christ, through whom we have gained access by faith into this grace in which we now stand. And we rejoice in the hope of the glory of God. . . .'[6] If we have come to God in repentance, confessing our sins, we will have been *justified*. Justified? Acquitted. Pardoned. Treated as if we had never sinned. Why? Because we will have accepted Jesus Christ as our Saviour from sin and, when God the Father looks at us, He will not see our life, but the sinless life of His Son. The issue in the judgement is not the sin question. It is the Son question. Our relationship with Jesus Christ.

If that relationship is ongoing, a day-by-day relationship, then we are, according to the Bible 'in Christ Jesus'. That being the case, we are 'complete in Him' — every step of the way, 'accepted in the Beloved', and 'there is therefore now no condemnation'.[7] ✠

In an uncertain world we can have a peace that passes understanding, a joy that no one can take from us — and the assurance of salvation.

Today God in Christ stretches out His hands to give us forgiveness for the past, an abundant life in the present, and a glorious hope for the future.

This is God's offer.

Whether we accept it is entirely up to us.

[1]John White, 'Channelling, a Short History of a Long Tradition', *Holistic Life Magazine* (Summer 1985), page 22. [2]*Gods of the New Age*, video (Riverside

Films 1984), Part 2. This is the logical extension of the political attitudes of the gurus and New Agers like Benjamin Creme. It is the fear of Fritz Haack and of a number of diplomats and academics — European and American — interviewed on this authoritative and objective documentary video. ³Luke 21:26-28, Phillips. ⁴1 Thessalonians 5:2, 3. ⁵Luke 17:26, 27. ⁶Romans 5:1, 2, NIV. ⁷Colossians 2:10; Ephesians 1:6; Romans 8:1.

Grace Awakening

What a contrast between God's great offer — and what New Age offers!

God's offer is called the Gospel.

God's Gospel brings emancipation from the dark forces of the occult world.

But before the Church can stand up against those dark forces — effectively present the Gospel to a society sliding into the dark realms of occultism — it must emancipate itself from the enemy within.

The enemy within?

Those who embrace the forms of Christianity but refuse to accept the power of God into their lives (2 Timothy 3:1-9).

And they are?

✧ Those who push Jesus into the once-a-week (if that) margins of their lives. Those who choose to live compromised lives. *Churchianity.* Remember? While they continue to predominate in our congregations the image they project will continue to be the image of the Church as a whole.

✧ Those who present to the world polythene packets of split hairs as a substitute for the Bread of Life. For, depend on it, 'split hairs' is how theology appears when it is debated by those whose lives have never been transformed by it. Properly understood, that is *cultism.*

✧ Those who, regardless of what they say, act as if personal performance — not the perfect performance of their Saviour — is their title to heaven. *Legalism* warps personalities because its end result is a life of hypocrisy and habitual sin.

✧ To survive, grow and evangelize, *the Christian* needs power. *Divine power;* the power of Christ and the Holy Spirit.

✧ To survive, grow and evangelize, *the Church* needs power. *Divine power;* the power of Christ and the Holy Spirit.

Winged thunderbolt

G. K. Chesterton described the apostolic church as 'a winged thunderbolt of everlasting enthusiasm'. Their message: the Lord crucified and risen; salvation and righteousness to be found only in Him. The centre of their worship: the Lord's table. Their mission: that every knee shall bow and every tongue confess that 'Jesus Christ is Lord'. Their hope: Maranatha — Lord, come!

The followers of Jesus had run from Gethsemane. At Calvary they had been conspicuous by their absence; and, in their hideaways, had been disillusioned, despondent and divided. Even after the resurrection Jesus had to chide them for their unwillingness to believe. But, within weeks, this group of men became, arguably, the most powerful force known to history.

What had made the difference?

The Spirit descended. The Spirit was the winged thunderbolt. When Jesus *ascended* to the throne at His Father's right hand, the Spirit *descended* to His throne. And the throne of the Spirit is the Church.

The end-time Church is back in the position of the infant Church: a micro-minority in a hostile society, fighting for its life once more. There is hostility and indifference without. And there is indifference and division within.

How do we evangelize in this hostile/indifferent world — when we are a divided/indifferent Church?

When persecution came to the infant Church it fell to Peter to stand up and defend it before the Sanhedrin. His defence — or was it *defiance?* — began with these words: 'We ought to obey God rather than men.'[1] First and foremost we must be certain of our authority. And that authority is the Bible and the Bible only.

The conclusion of Peter's defence is also of interest;

'*And we are his witnesses . . . and so is also the Holy Spirit.*'[2] Here are the two elements indispensable to successful end-time witness.

⟡ The apostolic witness; the message; the word.
⟡ The Holy Spirit to empower and confirm our witness.

These two elements must always go together.

In Christendom today there are two opposite emphases:

⟡ At one end we have groups who emphasize the first element, 'We are his witnesses.' The apostolic witness; the message of the Bible, orthodoxy.

⟡ At the other end are groups emphasizing that the only thing needful is the witness of the Spirit. They seem to be saying that it doesn't really matter what we believe so long as we have the powerful witness of the Spirit within.

Both extremes are wrong.

Unfortunately, it is possible to be perfectly orthodox — and perfectly dead. Today's snail's-pace church growth could be the result, not of inappropriate soul-winning techniques, but of the absence of the all-conquering power of the Holy Spirit.

Unfortunately the wing of the Church which has most to say about the Holy Spirit seems to be the place where confusion reigns, strange goings-on are rampant, and where there is the greatest disparity between profession and life-style.

The balance emphasized by Peter in Acts 5:32 must be maintained. The witness of the Church requires: ⟡ the Gospel; ⟡ the power of the Holy Spirit upon the Gospel.

On the night of His betrayal Jesus had urgent, final words for His disciples. Again and again in John's record of these final words (in John 13, 14, 15 and 16) Jesus kept returning to one theme. *He* was going away so that Another might come to empower them. The Power to come? The Spirit. The purpose of the Spirit? To testify to the power of Christ and His Gospel[3] Jesus emphasizes, 'He shall not speak of himself.' Hence when, after

Pentecost, the disciples were challenged with regard to their miracles, they did not preach about the experiences they were having in the Spirit. They preached Jesus crucified and risen. The witness of the Holy Spirit is to uplift Jesus.[4]

In short, then. The function of the Holy Spirit? To empower the Church to preach the Gospel.

Amazing grace

The great need of the Church is the need of revival. The need of revival is the need of the Spirit. And the Spirit will come in His fullness when the Church, once again, preaches the Gospel of grace.

The revival to come; *a grace awakening.*

The Gospel preached by Paul and the early apostles was the Gospel of salvation by grace through faith in Jesus Christ alone. We do not read of the apostles making political pronouncements, let alone of seeking political power and influence. We do, from time to time, read of them getting involved in peripheral issues. Often Paul took it upon himself to call them back to the Gospel of grace.

We find Paul doing this in his letter to the Galatians. The Gospel of grace, he told them, is a Gospel of freedom. Freedom from sin was only part of it. The other part? Freedom from religion! Religion is what *we* do; a system of salvation by track record, performance. The Gospel Paul preached was the good news of what God has done. Salvation, says Paul, is not through *performance*, but promise.[5] If we have accepted Jesus as our Saviour we are 'clothed with Christ'[6] and, once 'clothed with Christ', we are counted as sons of God *in Christ*. Once 'clothed with Christ', because of Calvary, everything that is legally Christ's (including salvation and eternal life) becomes ours — as long as we accept it. As God counts the Son, says Paul, so He counts us.

What a Gospel! And all made possible through grace.

And, as Paul found to his cost, whenever the Gospel of grace is preached, there is opposition — from *inside* the

Church! Opposition from what Charles Swindoll in his book *The Grace Awakening* (Word 1990) calls 'grace-busters'. Grace-busters (Pharisees) killed Jesus. Grace-busters (the Law Party) opposed Paul in Galatia. When the sixteenth-century reformers made grace their battle cry, grace-busters got angry, tied them to stakes and burned them alive. When John Wesley and George Whitfield led a grace awakening in eighteenth-century Britain, there were plenty of grace-busters to take their stand against them.

To allow the Spirit to work among us, as well as to open the way to our salvation, we need to both *live* and *preach* the Gospel of grace. Too many Christians are still bound and shackled by legalists' lists of dos and don'ts, held in the tight bondage dictated by those who have appointed themselves judge and jury over all. We need to give people permission to be free, absolutely free in Christ. And in this freedom in Christ is the complete antithesis to guruism, New Age.

Too many have been turned off by a twisted concept of the Christian life. This very twisted concept let in New Age. Instead of a winsome, contagious invitation to hope, peace, joy and salvation through the power of Christ, there have been too many Christians who have projected a grim-faced caricature of religion-on-demand. They have taken the freedom and fun out of faith.

Legalism has never worked. It has never produced the standards that it claims to uphold. The highest moral and spiritual achievements depend NOT upon *push*, but upon *pull*. And the 'pull power' comes as we fall on our knees at Calvary. At Calvary the law was magnified, justice was satisfied, sin was nullified, God was glorified, the sinner was justified and Satan was petrified.

Grace-busters carry a heavy disguise. Often they appear clean-cut, law-abiding types. But, with word, pen and look, they kill grace and freedom. No Christian church is without them. Their intolerance is tolerated. Their judgemental spirit remains unjudged. Their bullying tactics continue unchecked. And the great tragedy is this: Millions of

Christians, even now, are living their lives in shame, fear and intimidation — who *should* be free!

'From the fullness of his grace we have all received one blessing after another. For the law was given through Moses: grace and truth came through Jesus Christ.'[7] 'For it is by grace you have been saved. . . .'[8] What *is* grace? Grace is love that stoops. Grace is a kindness which, by definition, the recipient does not deserve and can never hope to earn. <u>And grace is absolutely and totally free.</u>

The Gospel is that Christ has come and died and thereby satisfied His Father's demands on sin, and that all we need to do is to claim His grace by accepting Him as our personal Saviour. That's amazing grace!

God helps the helpless, the undeserving, those who don't measure up. But He does so when we admit that we do not measure up. As we see the outworking of sin in the world, the New Age 'man-is-god' teaching is the most hideous of sick jokes. Because of sin we are all marred, spoiled, lost. We need redemption, re-creation, new birth. To claim those things we need to admit our need. Instead of striving for a man-made ticket to heaven based on high achievement and hard work (for which *we* get all the credit), the Gospel urges us to declare our own spiritual bankruptcy and accept God's free gift of grace.

<u>By</u> grace we receive *justification*. Justification? The sovereign act of God <u>whereby He declares righteous the believing sinner — receives him back into the fold as though he had never been away. Remember the prodigal son?</u>

No one is immune from the sin disease. But New Age doesn't even mention sin. The good news of the Gospel is that Jesus, the perfect Substitute, made the ultimate once-and-for-all payment on our behalf. It cost Him His life. As a result God gives the free gift of salvation to those who believe in His Son. Once we accept the seldom-announced fact that we have nothing to impress God with, we will be ready to accept His free gift.

There is one password to heaven: GRACE.

Wake up to grace! Grasp the truth about grace! Better still — grasp grace! Grasp grace, and God will give you the power to give up, to put on, to take off, to quit, to start — to *grow* in grace.

Wake up to grace!

Become part of a great grace awakening. Such a grace awakening would enable the Church to conquer the world.

There was never an Age of Pisces. There will never be an Age of Aquarius. But there are signs of a grace awakening within the Church. Elements of Christ's Gospel are coming together to explode into the greatest revival since Wesley, since Luther, since Paul, since Pentecost. When that revival occurs there will be a 'paradigm shift', more radical than either Renaissance or Reformation. *Then*, and only *then*, there will be a new world order. The new world order? God's Kingdom of Glory.

Meanwhile, by tapping into grace, tap into the power of God. Become part of the Grace Awakening.

---

[1]Acts 5:29. [2]Acts 5:32. [3]John 15:26; 16:13, 14. [4]Acts 2:24, *et seq.;* Acts 3:12, 13. [5]Galatians 3:10, 11. [6]Galatians 3:27, NIV. [7]John 1:16, 17, NIV. [8]Ephesians 2:8, NIV.